HOPES *and* DREAMS

HOPES *and* DREAMS

THE STORY OF BARACK OBAMA

STEVE DOUGHERTY

Photo Editor – Hal Buell

BLACK DOG
& LEVENTHAL
PUBLISHERS
NEW YORK

Published by Black Dog & Leventhal Publishers, Inc.
151 West 19th Street
New York, NY 10011

Research Assistant: Eva O. Dougherty

Book Design: Sheila Hart Design, Inc.

Cover photo: AP Photo/Chuck Kennedy, Pool Back cover photos: clockwise from top left: AP Photo/Ssg. Lorie Jewell HO; AP Photo/Stephan Savoia; AP Photo/Seth Wenig; AP Photo/Morry Gash; AP Photo/J. Scott Applewhite; AP Photo/Obama Presidential Campaign; AP Photo/Nam Y. Huh; AP Photo/Charles Rex Arbogast. Addiitonal photo credits can be found on page 192

ISBN-13: 978-1-57912-810-4

h g f e d c b a

Printed in the United States of America

CONTENTS

FOR WHOM HE SAVED THE UNION
THE MEMORY OF ABRAHAM LINCOLN
IS ENSHRINED FOREVER

HOPES *and* DREAMS

OBAMAMANIA

Before he formally launched his campaign for his party's nomination, seeking to become the first black president in American history, Obama—speaking to reporters after winning his 2004 Senate race (above right); celebrating his victory (above) with wife, Michelle, and daughters, Malia and Sasha; and on a campaign flight (right)—rallied Democrats to what he called his "new politics of hope."

I really tried to get Bono this weekend," Iowa senator Tom Harkin tells the cheering crowd at his annual Harkin Steak Fry at the Warren County Fairgrounds in Indianola, Iowa. "I settled for the second-biggest rock star in America."

With that, the headline attraction, a brown-eyed handsome man, takes the stage to giddy applause. But the swooning fans aren't going ga-ga just because Barack Obama has won more Grammy Awards (two) than Jimi Hendrix and Bob Marley combined (zero). He's getting the Elvis treatment simply because, as one fan, a young Republican named Veronica Czastkiewicz who drove three hours to catch his act, put it, "Barack's attitude is awesome. He's the only Democrat I'd vote for."

Ever since he wowed the world at the 2004 Democratic convention and won election to the U.S. Senate by a landslide that year, his fans couldn't resist comparing him to the supernovas of rock. "We originally scheduled the Rolling Stones for this party," New Hampshire governor John Lynch told a crowded hall of Barack-and-rollers at a rally in Manchester to celebrate the Democrats' November election victories. "But we

"There is not a liberal America and a conservative America. There is the United States of America."

BARACK OBAMA

In his star-making speech nominating John Kerry (with Kerry's wife, Teresa, and John Edwards, above right) at the 2004 Democratic Convention, Obama (with Michelle, right) first used the phrase that is the title of his best-selling book *The Audacity of Hope*. "In the end, that is God's greatest gift to us, the bedrock of this nation; the belief in things not seen; the belief that there are better days ahead."

cancelled them when we realized that Senator Obama would sell more tickets."

The sold-out rally and a second appearance in Portsmouth, New Hampshire, where he signed copies of his Oprah-endorsed best seller, *The Audacity of Hope,* attracted 2,500 people and the kind of media attention more likely to be found at the launch of a Stones tour than at a post-election Granite State political event. Some 150 members of the press, including sixty reporters and twenty-

Long-shot hopes are nothing new for Obama (left), a Chicago White Sox fan who celebrates at a rally in 2005, the year the perennial losers won their first World Series since 1917; he campaigns with his future 2008 primaries rival, John Edwards and Illinois senator Dick Durbin in 2004 (top left); Obama (above) stands in a Capitol Hill elevator after casting his vote on the nomination of Samuel Alito Jr. for Supreme Court justice in 2006.

two TV camera crews, covered Obama's visit to a state that would be the site of 2008's first presidential primary.

It was a scene repeated at an earlier series of stops around the country before the mid-term elections, as Obama launched a book tour that had all the trappings of something quite different.

"Sometimes a book tour is more than just a book tour," a former aide to Vice President Al Gore slyly noted as Obama crisscrossed

the country. At the first of three signings, on a single day in October, a woman in Chicago shouted "Obama for president!" as the senator arrived at a bookstore at 8:30 a.m. In San Rafael, California, an enterprising vendor did a brisk business selling homemade "Obama for President" buttons outside the Marin Civic Center, while 1,200 people turned out to hear him speak and wait in long lines to have him sign copies of *The Audacity of Hope*. The following day he was in Seattle where the largest single crowd on the tour, 2,500 people, attended a signing at Bellevue Community College. Audience members there held up the then-current issue of *Time* magazine with his face on the cover along with the words "Why Barack Obama Could Be the Next President."

"Senator Obama," Gore's former aide said, "appears to be using the book tour to really test presidential winds."

And so he was. Just three months later, on the morning after what would have been Martin Luther King Jr.'s seventy-eighth birthday, Obama filed papers with the Federal Election Commission, the first step in his quest to become the first black president in American history.

"Our vision of America is not one where a big government runs our lives; it's one that gives every American the opportunity to make the most of their lives."

BARACK OBAMA

"The decisions that have been made in Washington these past six years, and the problems that have been ignored, have put our country in a precarious place," he said in a videotaped message to supporters on January 16, 2007, explaining why he was entering the race. Citing voters' jitters about everything from their jobs to jihad and a "tragic and costly war that should never have been waged," Obama called for a new kind of politics to replace the present

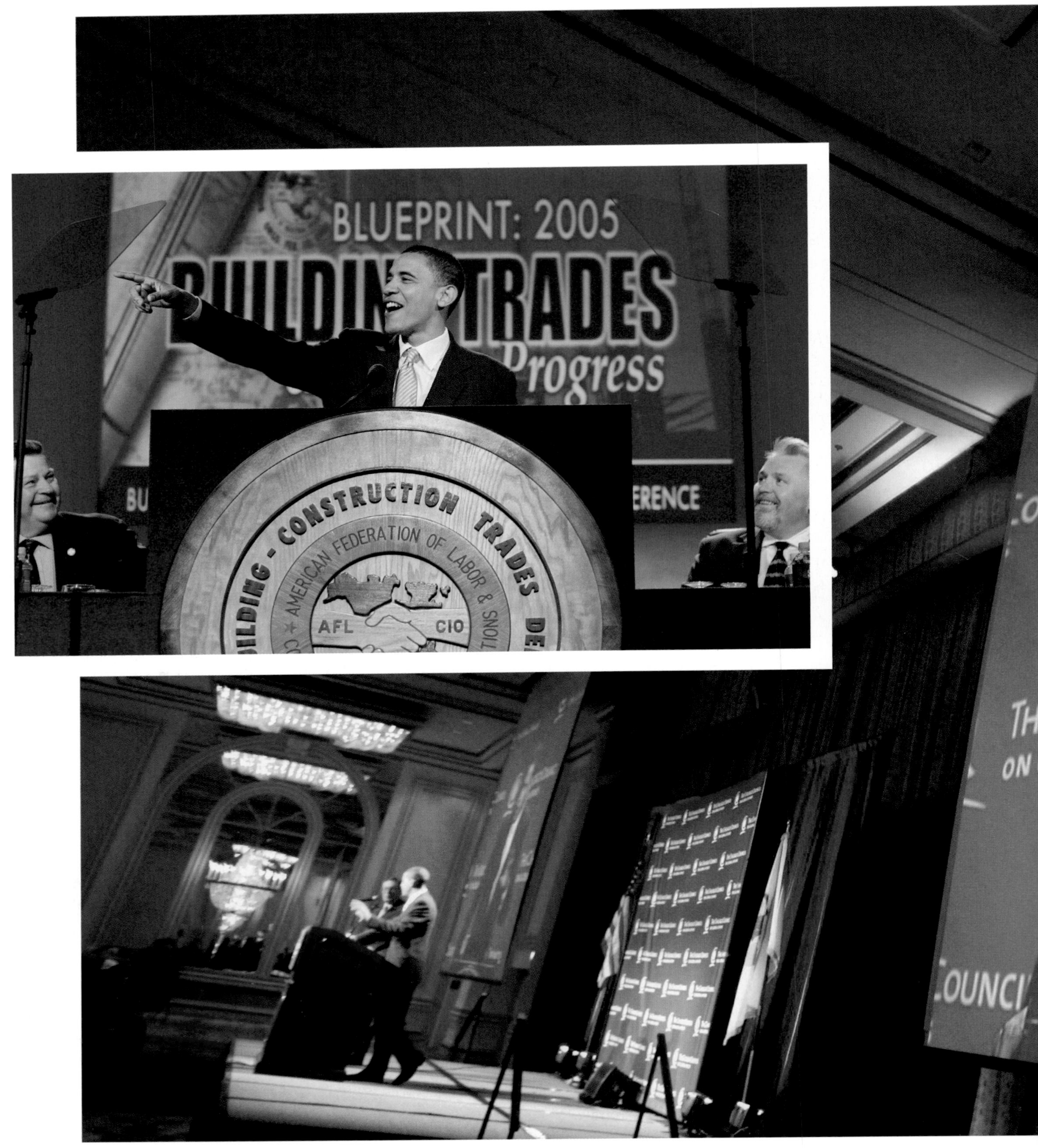
BLUEPRINT: 2005
TRADES
Progress
ERENCE
CONSTRUCTION
TRADES
AMERICAN FEDERATION OF LABOR &
AFL
CIO
COUNCI

Widely known in his homestate as an effective and innovative legislator during his seven years in the Illinois State Senate, Obama (inset) speaks at a 2005 Building Trades conference in Washington; and talks before the Chicago Council on Foreign Affairs in November 2006.

Obama speaks to the Chicago Council on Foreign Affairs in November 2005, calling for a reduction of troops in Iraq and criticizing the Bush adminstration for questioning the patriotism of those who speak against the war.

way of doing business in Washington. There, things are so "bitter and partisan, so gummed-up by money and influence," he said, "that we can't tackle the big problems that demand solutions."

In New Hampshire, two months before he filed Federal Election Commission papers, Obama's fans already seemed psyched for him to get in the race. Looking dapper and at ease in an open-collar white shirt and a black jacket, Obama was greeted by a sustained fusillade of camera flashes and standing ovations. In his smooth and rich baritone, he called for universal health care, energy independence, an effective policy to stem global warming, and an end to loud and uncivil, Limbaugh-like public discourse. "We've come to be consumed by a 24-hour, slash-and-burn, negative-ad, bickering, small-minded politics that doesn't move us forward," he said in Portsmouth, aiming his critique at both Republicans and his own party as they glowered across a gaping, ever-widening partisan gulf. "Sometimes one side is up, and the other side is down. But there's no sense that they are coming together in a common-sense, practical, nonideological way to solve the problems that we face."

"It's just not my style to go out of my way to offend people or be controversial just for the sake of being controversial. That's offensive and counterproductive. It makes people feel defensive and more resistant to changes."

BARACK OBAMA

The call to overcome the great American cultural and partisan divide is a central theme of both his book *The Audacity of Hope* and his campaign. In times of trouble, when despair and anger may seem the only alternatives, he said, in keeping with the book's campaign-ready message, "what's hard, what's risky, what's truly audacious, is to hope."

Angered by the Bush administration's reponse to Hurricane Katrina, Obama (at a Habitat for Humanity project in New Orleans in July 2006, right), said the government "was so detached from the realities of inner-city life in New Orleans...they couldn't conceive of the notion that [residents] couldn't load up their SUVs...and drive off to a hotel with a credit card." Below Obama listens during an October 2006 campaign rally for Ohio gubernatorial candidate Ted Strickland.

Obama's early and eloquent speeches against the war in Iraq in 2002 (he said the looming invasion was an ill-conceived venture that would "require a U.S. occupation of undetermined length, at undetermined cost, with undetermined consequences") lifted the then-obscure Illinois legislator to statewide prominence and paved the way

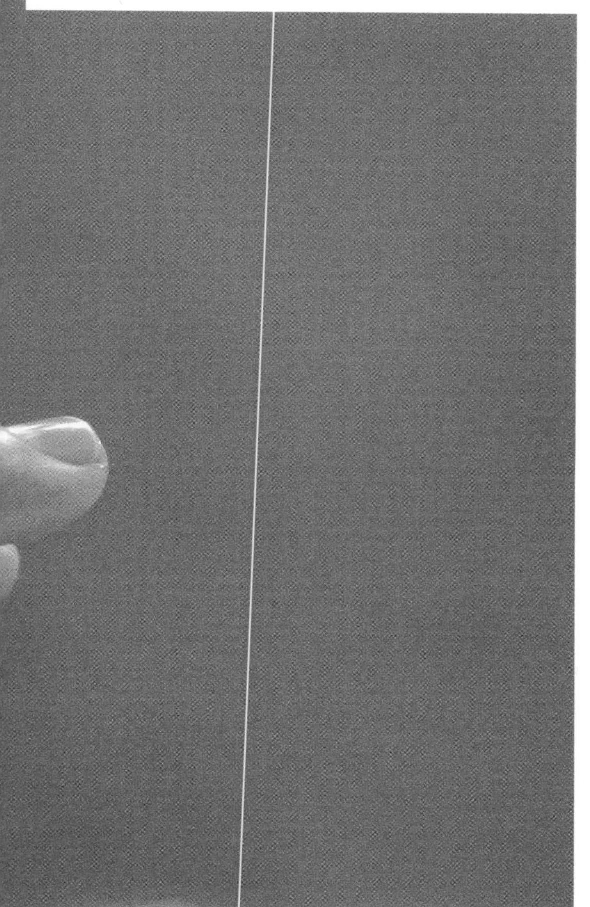

"What's hard, what's risky, what's truly audacious, is to hope."

BARACK OBAMA

for his march to the Senate. In Portsmouth he renewed his call for the redeployment of American troops in Iraq. "We can't just waste our most precious resource—our young men and women," he told the crowd. The words prompted one listener, a Republican whose son recently returned from his second tour of duty, to tell a reporter, "If he runs [he didn't need to say for what], I'll help."

"He had the true spirit we're looking for," said one member of the audience who was reminded not of a rock star but of one of an earlier generation's most revered political figures. "I haven't been so excited by someone since JFK when he was campaigning when I was ten years old."

"I've never seen anything like it," echoed a former New Hampshire lawmaker who, as he watched Obama electrify a crowd of normally subdued Democratic Party supporters, was reminded of another Kennedy. "A lot of people have compared it to the days when Bobby Kennedy was running for president. I don't think we've seen it since."

Jack or Bobby: to be equated with either is heady stuff for any politician but especially a first-term senator with presidential ambitions. Obama's youth, energy and idealism, not to mention his athletic good looks, have inspired memories of—and

comparisons to—both brothers.

The first president born in the 20th century, Jack Kennedy was, like Obama, young, charismatic, and—yes—even sexy.

In Manchester, Obama echoed President Kennedy's call for a New Frontier: "America is ready to turn the page," he said. "America

"I have no interest in being the un-Hillary," said Obama, whose early opposition to what he calls "the fiasco in Iraq" gained him the support of many Democrats angered by his campaign rival's long-stated support for the war. Even so, he said of Clinton (with Obama in July 2006), "I think she'd be a capable president."

is ready for a new set of challenges. This is our time. A new generation is prepared to lead."

But it is the younger Kennedy that draws the most comparisons. Like Obama, Bobby was a witty, eloquent, dashing, and politically progressive, forty-something freshman junior senator from a large northern industrial state when he ran for president in 1968. Bobby sat at the same desk Obama was assigned when he first joined the Senate and was sworn in on January 4, 1965, forty years to the day before his political descendant. Bobby also launched his quest as the electorate was despairing under the rising death count of a badly conceived and ill-defined, no-end-in-sight war. Then the nation longed for a return to Camelot, the brief, however illusory, flowering of optimism that preceded the bitter divisiveness and culture wars that are still with us.

However, the road to political glory is littered with nearly as many supposedly Kennedy-esque political rock stars (Dan Quayle, Jack Kemp anyone? Paging John Edwards!) as Fab Fours and Fives whose sure-thing route to stardom ended the moment they were cast as the next Beatles. Perhaps realizing the risks involved, Obama is wise not to fit himself for the Kennedy mantle. Even so, he frequently cites Bobby Kennedy as one of his political heroes, along with other American martyrs JFK, Abraham Lincoln, and Martin Luther King Jr.

"Barack represents change and hope," a former Clinton White House political director said of Obama, here talking on a cell phone outside the Senate chamber in April 2006. "There are moments in our country—1960 was one of them—when people are looking for more and are willing to take a chance on [a candidate's potential for] greatness."

In a sad irony, the fortieth anniversary of King's and RFK's deaths by assassins' bullets would be observed at the height of the 2008 presidential election campaign. And reportedly, Obama's wife, Michelle, cited her fears for her husband's security when she argued initially against his running. Those fears were underscored when Obama was assigned secret service protection earlier than any other candidate.

"Everywhere he goes, people want him to run for president, especially in Iowa, cradle of presidential contenders. Around here, they're even naming babies after him."

TERRY MORAN, ABC'S *NIGHTLINE*, DURING HIS PROFILE OF OBAMA

"I was only seven when Bobby Kennedy died," Obama said in an address during the Robert F. Kennedy Human Rights Award Ceremony in Washington in 2005, when Kennedy would have celebrated his eightieth birthday. "I knew him only as an icon."

And yet, when Obama invokes Kennedy in his speeches, he sounds as if he could be reading a passage from his own book. "In a nation torn by war and divided against itself," he said in tribute to RFK, "he was able to look us in the eye and tell us that no matter...how persistent the poverty or the racism, no matter how far adrift America strayed, hope would come again."

Like Kennedy, Obama had been a celebrated figure and a beacon of hope for his party before he first stepped foot into the

Senate chamber and took a seat at his predecessor's desk to become the upper house's third black senator since Reconstruction—and its sole, current African American member.

His election victory in November 2004 ignited the near-hysteria known as Obamamania that his supporters hope will carry him all the way to the White House. When he and his wife caught a screening of the film *Ray* at a theater near his home in Hyde Park, on the South Side of Chicago, shortly after the election, audience members clapped and cheered as he took his seat. Mobbed by the media and by passersby on the streets

"He's the star. He is in such demand. He's in greater demand than any other person that we have to offer."

SEN. CHARLES SCHUMER

Obama "is the most galvanizing leader to come out of either party in at least a decade," said Ben Affleck. Among other celeb Obamamaniacs are Tom Cruise and Katie Holmes (with Michelle Obama, left), George Clooney (above), and another rock star, Bono (right); the Obamas attend the 2005 NAACP Image Awards (top right).

FOX
NAACP
IMAGE
AWARDS

"I miss them terribly and miss Michelle terribly," Obama (with his family in March 2004) said of life on the campaign trail. "I'm just blessed that Michelle is so good with the children and so well organized that she's really been able to take care of home base."

of Chicago and Washington where fans of all ages and ethnic stripes shouted his name, clapped him on the back, and asked him for autographs and to pose for snapshots, Obama found himself at the center of the kind of adulation usually reserved for sports heroes, or movie and—of course—rock stars. Swooning press reports led a waggish *Chicago Reader* writer to note that "No Chicago pol has heard this kind of flattery since an alderman compared Richard J. Daley to Jesus Christ."

"That would be my favorite guy. . . I would hope that he would run for president."

OPRAH WINFREY

Appearances on innumerable talk shows and magazine covers spread his image throughout the land, and his place in the pop firmament was confirmed in an episode of *Will & Grace* when Grace dreamed she showered with the man whom she said was "Barack-ing my world!"

"I'm so overexposed I make Paris Hilton look like a recluse," the senator-elect quipped at the Gridiron Club Dinner in December 2004 a month before he took office. "I figure there's nowhere to go from here but down, so tonight I'm announcing my retirement from the United States Senate."

With the words of Obama's stirring convention speech from the summer before still ringing in their ears and tallies of his landslide victory fresh in their minds (he won over 70 percent of the vote in a state where the electorate is only 15 percent black), Democrats began fantasizing about getting him to run in 2008, if not for president, at least vice president. While *Newsweek* termed such talk "almost comically premature for an incoming senator," the magazine also pointed out that Obama, then forty-three, was "the same age JFK was when he was elected president."

A few short years before, the notion that Obama would be "the man…more and more people are saying could be America's first black president," as the host introduced him on *Larry King Live* last October, would not have seemed comical; it simply wouldn't have crossed anyone's mind, least of all Obama's. "Oprah herself wants him to run!" rang out King in near-endorsement.

In *The Audacity of Hope*, Obama recalls that when he attended his first Democratic Convention, in Los Angeles in 2000, he was at the nadir of his political career. Three years after being elected to the Illinois state senate, he made what he now concedes was a hasty and ill-advised attempt to run for Congress in 1999. Critics called it a disaster.

Obama ran against Bobby Rush, a former Black Panther Party member and four-term congressman who enjoyed wide popularity in his overwhelmingly black South Side district in Chicago. Obama endured thinly veiled suggestions that his light-colored skin, his law degree, and his biracial lineage—no descendant of slaves, his father was a government official from Kenya, his mother a Kansas-born WASP—meant that he was elitist and not "black enough" to relate to the lives and needs of the constituents. Rush trounced him by a two-to-one margin in the primary. Obama retreated to his law practice at a small civil rights firm in Chicago. He had, he wrote in *Hope,* "left the practice unattended during the campaign (a neglect that had left [him] more or less broke)."

"Run, Barack, run. Barack Obama should run for president. He should run first for the good of his party. It would demoralize the Democrats to go through a long primary season with the most exciting figure in the party looming off in the distance like some unapproachable dream."

DAVID BROOKS, *THE NEW YORK TIMES*

Just how broke he spells out in his book. After his defeat, he was cajoled by friends to attend the 2000 Democratic Convention in L.A. "Although they didn't say this at the time," he writes, "I suspect they saw a trip to the convention as a bit of useful therapy for me, on the theory that the best thing to do after getting thrown off a horse is to get back on right away." When he landed in L.A., his American Express card was rejected at the Hertz counter. "After half an hour on the phone, a kindhearted supervisor at American Express authorized the car rental," he writes. "But the episode served as an omen of things to come." Without credentials as a delegate and no floor passes available, he ended up watching the proceedings on televisions set up inside the Staples Center. He left the convention without witnessing the coronation of Al Gore as the Democratic standard-bearer. And he left with scant hope for the future of his political career.

"Dick Cheney and Donald Rumsfeld have an awful lot of experience."

OBAMA, ON THOSE WHO QUESTION HIS QUALIFICATIONS FOR HIGHER OFFICE.

The memory of that experience, and of the electoral slapdown that preceded it, left him with an indelible "sense of how fleeting fame is." It was, he writes, "the sort of drubbing that awakens you to the fact that life is not obliged to work out as you'd planned."

It also equipped him to see the foolishness of believing what he calls "the hyperbole" lavished upon him in the wake of his rousing speech at that other, happier convention four years later and following his election victory in 2004. "It was my first day in the [Senate office] building," he writes of a press conference he held on the day before his swearing-in 2005. "I had not taken a single vote, had not introduced a single bill—indeed I had not even sat down at my desk—when a very earnest reporter raised his hand and asked, 'Senator Obama, what is your place in history?'

"Even some of the other reporters had to laugh."

No one was laughing two years later as he answered the drumbeat of supporters calling upon him to launch his candidacy and take his place in history. There were, however, plenty who scoffed that Obama was too young, too inexperienced, and, yes, too black to win in 2008.

Supporters like Illinois Senate President Emil Jones Jr. countered by touting Obama's color-blind appeal. He described encounters like the one he had during the 2004 U.S. Senate campaign when an eighty-six-year-old downstate white woman said, "I hope I live long enough because this young man's going to be president and I want to be able to vote for him!" *Chicago Sun-Times* columnist Laura Washington by contrast, quoted her uncle Leland "Sugar" Cain, who said he was a fan of Obama's but did not think whites will elect him president. "When it's time to go into the voting booth," Cain told his niece, "they're not going to pull that lever."

New York magazine writer John Heilemann agreed, but argued that race is not the main issue. "Obamamaniacs must be smoking something," he quipped. "For all his promise, Obama is basically an empty

vessel, with vulnerabilities that have been obscured by his blinding, meteoric ascent."

A member of the Trinity United Church of Christ in Chicago who keeps a Bible in his car, Obama (in a prayerful moment at his church in 2004) has never been a Muslim, as some Rightist talk-radio critics have rumored. Remarks made by the church pastor would cause a crisis late in the primary season.

Like a critic puncturing the bubble of the biggest, best-selling rock star's most popular hit, Heilemann belittled the oft-heard comparisons of Obama to Bobby Kennedy, saying the differences between them "are many, beginning with the length and depth of their résumés....Obama's... pales by comparison."

"The excitement he's generated isn't issue-based: it's stylistic," wrote Heilemann, who wondered "how well this brand of popularity will hold up when voters learn more about him...such as the fact that he's a smoker."

Heilemann meant cigarettes. (Obama, trying to quit, was down to puffing three a day). But when Jay Leno asked him in December 2006 if he smoked, he was talking not about Marlboros but about pot.

While he has cosponsored many bills with Republicans as a minority party member in both the Illinois and U.S. Senates, Obama (at his office on Capitol Hill in 2006, above, and with Karl Rove, right) decries Rove's polarizing tactics. At left, Obama speaks at a Summer Intern Town Hall meeting in Washington, 2006.

"In this new economy, teaching our kids just enough so that they can get through Dick and Jane isn't going to cut it."

BARACK OBAMA

Obama had admitted to smoking it in *Dreams from My Father*, a searingly honest and soul-searching memoir written years before he ever considered a political career. Little noticed when it was first published in 1995, it spent a year on the *New York Times* best-seller list when it was reissued in the wake of his political success in 2004. It also won Obama a Grammy for Best Spoken Word Album in 2006. (He won his second Grammy in 2008 for his recorded reading of *Audacity of Hope*.) In a preface to the

new edition he said that he would not "tell the story much differently today than I did ten years ago, even if certain passages have proven to be inconvenient politically."

> **"I am suspicious of hype."**
>
> BARACK OBAMA

"Not recently—this was in high school," Obama said in response to Leno's question.

"Did you inhale?" Leno said, alluding to Bill Clinton's famous dodge.

"That was the point," Obama said.

A group of pundits and political analysts quoted in a January 3, 2007, *Washington Post* story said they believe that Obama's disarming candor made it a dead issue. "Americans have an appetite for redemption," said one Republican consultant. "Who's going to cast the first stone?" asked a Democratic counterpart.

Obama didn't excise the passages about drug use from his book—he also said that he tried cocaine as well—because, perhaps, as he said during his Senate campaign, he felt it was important for "young people who are already in circumstances far more difficult than mine [were] to know that you can make mistakes and still recover.

"At this stage in my life," he said, "my life is an open book, literally and figuratively. Voters can make a judgment as to whether dumb things that I did when I was a teenager are relevant to the work that I've done since that time."

One conundrum Obama faces is as inescapable as it is impossible to measure for its effect on voters—his name. In *The Audacity of Hope*, he recounts a meeting with a media consultant to discuss his political future. "As it happened, the lunch was scheduled for late September 2001.

"'You realize, don't you, that the political dynamics have changed,'" the consultant said. "We both looked down at the newspaper beside him," Obama writes. "There on the front page was Osama bin Laden.

"'Hell of a thing, isn't it?...You can't change your name, of course. Voters are suspicious of that kind of thing. Maybe if you were at the start of your career, you know, you could use a nickname or something. But now...'"

Name recognition for any politician is the coin of the realm, but for Obama it seemed a curse. He despaired for a time, imagining it signaled the end of his political career. "I began feeling," he writes, "the way I imagine an actor or athlete must feel when, after years of commitment to a particular dream, after years of waiting tables between auditions or scratching out hits in the minor leagues, he realizes that he's gone just about as far as talent or fortune will take him."

After seriously considering abandoning politics for a "calmer, more stable, and better-paying existence," he writes, "at some point I arrived at acceptance—of my limits, and, in a way, my mortality...And it was this acceptance, I think, that allowed me to come up with the thoroughly cockeyed idea of running for the United States Senate."

His supporters can point to it as a testament to his character that he saw the name he inherited from his father, Barack Hussein Obama—triply toxic as it would become with the coming of both Saddam and Borat—as just another obstacle to overcome in pursuit of his own "particular

While Obama (in his Senate office, top) relies on staff to handle scheduling and other nuts-and-bolts campaign needs, his closest adviser is himself. "In terms of what's important to the country," he said, "I think my instincts are good. I trust them." At right, Obama prepares for an appearance on his friend Oprah Winfrey's television show in 2006.

dream." While Obama seldom if ever uses the middle name, he apparently has instructed his staff to be forthright about it. When a reporter called his office in Washington last year and gingerly asked the correct spelling of the senator's middle name, a staffer said simply, "Like the dictator."

As deftly as he has managed to defuse the jarring associations attached to his name—Barack means "blessed" in Swahili, he tells audiences; and he invariably gets laughs when he says that people are always hearing Obama as "Alabama" or "Yo Mama"—it has dogged him steadily. Jan Schakowsky, a member of

"He's ready. Why wait? Obama '08."

BUMPER STICKER SEEN ALL OVER WASHINGTON, D.C.

Illinois's congressional delegation has said that when President Bush glimpsed her Obama button during a White House visit in 2004, "He jumped back, almost literally. And I knew what he was thinking. So I reassured him it was Obama, with a 'b'."

Schakowsky explained that Obama was a Chicagoan running for the U.S. Senate.

"Well, I don't know him," Bush said.

"But you will, Mr. President," she replied.

"[L]et's face it," Obama said as he began the speech that electrified the 2004 Democratic Convention and that can still inspire the tears of believers, even on the written page, "my presence on this stage is pretty unlikely. My father was a foreign student, born and raised in a small village in Kenya. He grew up herding goats, went to school in a tin-roof shack. His father, my grandfather, was a cook, a domestic servant....Through

Obama stands at George W. Bush's side after the president signed into law the Federal Funding Accountability and Transparency Act of 2006, a bill cosponsored by Obama and Sen. Tom Coburn, a Republican from Oklahoma.

hard work and perseverance my father got a scholarship to study in a magical place, America, which stood as a beacon of freedom and opportunity to so many who had come before. While studying here, my father met my mother. She was born in a town on the other side of the world, in Kansas...My parents shared not only an improbable love; they shared an abiding faith in the possibilities of this nation. They would give me an African name, Barack, or 'blessed,' believing that in a tolerant America your name is no barrier to success...I stand here knowing that my story is part of the larger American story, that I owe a debt to all of those who came before me, and that, in no other country on earth is my story even possible."

Now he stands on an even larger stage. And Obama's story—of how, as he likes to say, "a tall, skinny kid with big ears," who came from nowhere in the continental United States, who grew up in Hawaii, forever an outsider, a black kid abandoned at age two by his father and, for long periods, his mother, raised by her parents in a white neighborhood and looked at askance by all of a more definable hue and tribe, who struggled mightily to find an identity and a purpose in life, has risen to become a candidate for president of the United States and a voice whose call for a union undivided by liberal and conservative, red state and blue, or black and white, springs from his own struggles to find a way to unite his own divided heart—seems all the more unlikely.

YOUNG BARRY

"Come to us, Obama!" crowds waving American flags chanted in Kisumu (right) in 2006 when Obama was also welcomed to his late father's home by villagers in Kogelo (top right) and visited with his step-grandmother, Sarah Hussein Onyango Obama (above).

The first time he arrived in Kenya in 1987, Obama was a twenty-six-year-old Chicago community organizer preparing to enter Harvard Law School. He landed at the airport to find that his luggage had been lost en route and he roared into Nairobi in an aunt's beat-up Volkswagen Beetle with a knocking engine and no muffler.

Later, on his way to his ancestral village of Kogelo, in rural western Kenya—the land immortalized in Hemingway's *Green Hills of Africa*—he took an all-night train to the town of Kisumu and rode from there for hours in an overcrowded and rickety jitney-like matatu with bald tires and few seats. On his lap during the bumpy ride were his half sister Auma, a squealing baby that a stranger asked him to hold, and a basket full of yams. It was not exactly as he had often fantasized his visit to the land of his father—as a "homecoming ... clouds lifting, old demons fleeing, the earth trembling as ancestors rose up in celebration."

Nineteen years later, that fantasy seemed to come true before his eyes. When Obama, his wife—Michelle—and their two daughters, Malia and Sasha, landed at Nairobi's

"When my tears were finally spent," wrote Obama—shown with Sarah in Kogelo (bottom) and watering an African olive tree in Nairobi with his two daughters and, in yellow, Nobel peace laureate Wangari Maathai —of his 1987 visit to his father's grave, "I felt a calmness wash over me. I felt the circle finally close."

Kenyatta International Airport in the summer of 2006, the U.S. ambassador met their plane, and they were whisked past a throng of waiting reporters and ferried into town in a twelve-car motorcade.

Rapturous crowds of Kenyans wearing T-shirts emblazoned with his name and likeness chanted "Come to us, Obama!" as he visited a memorial at the site of the U.S. embassy bombing in Nairobi.

Foregoing the all-night train ride, Obama and his family flew to Kisumu where thousands lined the route to Kogelo, many climbing trees for a better view of the motorcade carrying the American that the local Luo tribespeople loudly claimed as their own. "He's our brother," said one. "He's our son."

In Kogelo, the tiny village where Obama's father and grandfather are buried side by side and where the octogenarian Luo he calls "Granny" still lives, crowds chanted his name, a tribal singer sang his praises, and children sang songs they had composed in his honor. A villager offered him a present "to signify our appreciation"—a three-year-old goat led on a tattered rope leash. "It is very fat," he said, "and very sweet." Obama politely declined and shared a meal of chicken, porridge, and cabbage with his wife and kids, Auma—who acted as interpreter for their Granny, who spoke only Luo—and other relatives.

"Even though I had grown up on the other side of the world," Obama said to villagers of his visit nineteen years before, "I felt the spirit among the people who told me that I belonged."

"There's a core decency to the American people that doesn't get enough attention."

BARACK OBAMA

He had embarked on that journey uneasily, however. He was, he wrote in *Dreams from My Father* (the literary memoir that chronicles his coming of age), "a Westerner not entirely at home in the West, an African on his way to a land full of strangers."

Once there, however, he began to feel the sense of transformation that friends back home had described after their first visits to Africa. "For a span of weeks or months," he wrote, "you could experience the freedom that comes from not feeling watched, the freedom of believing that your hair grows as it's supposed to grow and that your rump sways the way a rump is supposed to sway ...Here the world was black, and so you were just you."

Until that maiden voyage to Africa, a rite of passage that helped him reconcile the world he grew up in and the world of a father he never really knew, he endured a long and often-painful struggle to understand who he truly was.

It was, he would recall, "a ten-year-old's nightmare." It was 1971, and he had just been introduced to the classroom on his first day of school at Honolulu's Punahou School by a kindly teacher with the nice name of Miss Hefty, who heard giggles when she used his full name.

"I thought your name was Barry," said a boy he'd met when his grandfather escorted him to school that morning.

"Barack is such a beautiful name," said Miss Hefty, who had lived in Kenya herself and had been delighted to learn that the new boy's father was Kenyan. "It's such a magnificent country. Do you know what tribe your father is from?"

When Obama quietly replied, "Luo," another boy hooted like a monkey, causing

Living in a two-bedroom apartment on the tenth floor of a building in one of the less-fashionable neighborhoods in glitzy Honolulu (left), Obama was admitted to the elite Punahou School (below right and left) at age ten after his grandfather's boss, an alumnus, used his clout to help get him in. Obama with his mother Ann Dunham (bottom far left) in an undated photo from the 1960's.

"I found that I've never learned anything from refusing to listen to other people or refusing to engage in conversation with them, and that surely can't be the basis for healthy politics in our society."

BARACK OBAMA

Obama's mother, Ann Dunham (with his Indonesian stepfather, Lolo Soetoro, and half sister Maya Soetoro), insisted that he supplement his schooling by taking U.S. correspondence courses during the four years he lived in Indonesia. Ann woke him at 4:00 a.m. every morning to instruct him for three hours before he left for school and she went to her job at the American embassy. After Barrack Hussein Obama, Sr. (right) spent the Christmas holidays with his then 10-year-old son in Hawaii, where Obama was living with his white grandparents, father and son never met again.

the whole class to break up in laughter. Before the day was out, a red-haired girl asked if she could touch his hair, and a boy asked him if his father was a cannibal.

"The novelty of having me in class quickly wore off for the other kids," Obama would later write. His fellow students, mostly the privileged children of well-off families who lived in houses far grander than the two-bedroom apartment Obama shared with his mother's parents, weren't overtly cruel. They didn't beat him up or mock him. They simply lost interest in the black kid who played soccer, badminton, and chess—games he'd learned from his Indonesian stepfather while living in Jakarta with his mother for four years before returning to Hawaii without her—but who couldn't throw a football or ride a skateboard.

As the months passed, he managed to make a few friends and "to toss a wobbly football around," but mostly he withdrew into a routine of going home after school, reading comics, watching TV, and listening to the radio. "I felt safe," he wrote; "it was as if I had dropped into a long hibernation."

He was shocked out of it a few months after school began when his grandparents on his mother's side ("Gramps" and "Toot," short for *tutu*, the Hawaiian word for grandmother) announced that his father and namesake—who Obama had not seen since he was only months old—was coming for a visit at Christmas. Also coming home for the holidays was his mother, Ann, flying in from Jakarta with Obama's half-sister, Maya. "Should be one hell of a Christmas," Gramps said.

Years later Obama would write that while growing up, "my father remained a myth to me, both more and less than a man," a figure he knew only through the stories his mother and grandparents told and the memories, almost always fond, that they shared with him. In their stories Barack Sr. was tall and handsome, gracious and wise; he spoke in a deep baritone with a lilting British accent; he had a strong singing voice, full of personality, and he was an excellent dancer; he was both powerful and kind, honest and frank—traits that could make him seem "a bit domineering" and "uncompromising sometimes," his mother admitted. He was brilliant of mind, a Phi Beta Kappa, and charming and self-confident.

"It's a fact, Bar," Gramps said. "Your dad could handle any situation, and that made everybody like him."

In family photographs, Obama saw his father's "dark laughing face, the prominent forehead, and thick glasses that made him appear older than his years."

From his mother he learned that his father was born on the shores of Lake Victoria in a poor village where his father, Hussein Onyango Obama, was a learned elder of their tribe, and a healer and medicine man. He taught his son to tend his herd of goats and to know the value of a good education, sending him to a local school run by the British colonial administration. Barack Sr. attended college in Nairobi on scholarship, and as Kenya prepared for independence, he was chosen to go to America to continue his education so that he could return and become a leader who would help build the fledgling nation.

In 1959 Obama's father, then twenty-three, became the first African student at the University of Hawaii. There, in a Russian-language class, Barack the elder, who, his son would write, was "black as pitch," met a cheerful, wide-eyed, eighteen-year-old freshman who was by contrast "white as milk."

Ann Dunham was the Kansas-born daughter of a furniture store manager and life insurance salesman who harbored a bohemian streak—he wrote poetry and listened to jazz.

"I've got relatives who look like Bernie Mac and I've got relatives who look like Margaret Thatcher. So we've got it all."

BARACK OBAMA

His more pragmatic wife was the punctual employee of a local bank whose family back in Kansas could trace a branch of its lineage to a famous ancestor—Jefferson Davis, president of the Confederate States of America.

The Dunhams had moved to the islands the year after Barack Sr. The two began dating and after a brief courtship, wed—an act that in 1960 was a crime in most states. "In many parts of the South," Obama would write, "my father could have been strung up from a tree for merely looking at my mother the wrong way."

Newly admitted to the Union, however, Hawaii was young and relatively tolerant, and the family history includes no accounts of Obama's parents suffering abuse on the streets of Honolulu. His father earned his degree in economics in just three years, graduating in 1962, the year after his son was born.

Offered a generous graduate-study scholarship at the New School in New York that would have allowed him to bring his wife and son with him to the city, Obama Sr. accepted instead a tuition-only grant from Harvard. He believed he said that a Ph.D. from that world-famous institution would strengthen the portfolio he would carry with him when he returned to Kenya and took up whatever position of leadership awaited him.

Moving to Boston alone, he and Ann agreed that she and the baby would join him when his studies were complete and together they would move back to Kenya as a family.

Time and distance eroded the relationship, however, and the couple eventually divorced. Whatever memories their toddler had of his father dissolved as well.

His mother remarried and in 1967 she moved with her son and new husband, Lolo Soetoro, who was also a graduate of the University of Hawaii, to Soetoro's homeland of Indonesia, where Obama lived for four years.

As he grew older, Obama was told that his father had returned, alone, to Kenya after earning his degree at Harvard. There

A distant relative through Obama's mother's family, Confederate president Jefferson Davis (top left) would no doubt be surprised to know that the young batsman at right would grow up to run for president of the Union that Davis warred with over the issue of slavery.

he became an economist and an important figure in the administration of the new nation. He also remarried and had five children. Those children—four boys and a girl, Barack's mother told him—were his half brothers and sister, his family in Africa.

As Obama would learn many years later, almost everything he knew about his father was a myth.

"He is a voice of strength and moderation, an American success story."

SEN. JOHN McCAIN ON OBAMA

His father's monthlong holiday visit to Hawaii in 1971 was painfully awkward at first, filled with long silences and disappointments. His father had recently been in a car accident and walked with a limp and a cane; he was thinner than Barack expected and he looked fragile; his eyes had a yellowy sheen, a lingering but unmistakable sign that he had a history of malaria. When his father ordered him to turn off the television—"He has been watching that machine constantly and now it is time for him to study!" he commanded—Barack ran to his room and slammed the door.

When Miss Hefty had invited his father to speak at his school, Barack panicked. He had bragged to his friends that his grandfather was a tribal chief, "like the king," and his father was the prince; he himself, he hinted, was next in line after his father to lead the Luo—a "tribe...of warriors," he said; the family name, Obama, he added, "means 'Burning Spear.'"

As much as he dreaded that his exaggerations would be exposed as lies, he listened enthralled along with his classmates and teachers as his father spoke vividly and eloquently about Kenya and its people and history. When he finished to much applause, a teacher told Barack "You've got a pretty impressive father."

"Your dad," said a classmate, the boy who had asked on the first day of school if his father ate people, "is pretty cool."

After that, he warmed up to his father. They attended a Dave Brubeck concert and

After his grandfather took him to see a University of Hawaii basketball game, Obama (third from left, second row, with Punahou's junior varsity team in 1977) practiced for hours a day alone on a playground near his apartment.

his father gave him a basketball for Christmas. They walked around the city, and his father introduced him to old friends from college. They lay side by side on his father's bed, reading together. On the day he left, he gave Barack two records of African music that he had brought from Kenya as a present.

"Come on Barry," his father said as the record played on Gramps's stereo. "You will learn from the master."

With that his father began to sway to the music, his arms "swinging as they cast an invisible net," his head back, his eyes closed, his "hips moving in a tight circle…he [let] out a quick shout, bright and high."

He would always remember the sound of that shout. While he would exchange letters with his father and dream about him through the years, he would never see him again.

Soon after his father returned to Kenya, Obama left his grandparents' apartment and moved in with his mother, who had seperated from her second husband and resettled in Hawaii to study for her masters in anthropology.

He grew close to his mother and half-sister during the three years he lived with Ann and Maya. Her ideals, forged in the 1960s and stirred by the civil rights movement, formed him. Ann drilled her values into him, Obama writes: "tolerance, equality, standing up for the disadvantaged." When Obama was 13, Ann urged him to return to Indonesia with her and Maya, where Ann planned to do the field-work necessary for her degree. He refused.

He told his mother that it was because he had grown to like his school and he didn't want to be cast as the new kid again, once more the stranger, proving himself in yet another foreign world.

But the real reason, he wrote, was that he had become "engaged in a fitful interior struggle" to forge his identity, to come to grips with a basic fact of his life, that he was "a black man in America," but one with no model, no father, to learn from.

Living once again in his old bedroom in his grandparents' apartment, he settled into the universal teenage routine of school, part-time jobs, and coping with, he wrote, "turbulent desire."

Years later, when Obama was a candidate for the U.S. Senate, he told a reporter that when he was in the 7th grade, he "was such a terror that my teachers didn't know what to do with me."

His sister, now married and living in Honolulu, told *Time* that in high school, Barack "had powers. [H]e was charismatic,"

said Maya Soetoro-Ng. "He had lots of friends" and such a way with women that he would go to the University of Hawaii campus to "meet university ladies."

Throughout his junior high and high school years, he tried to glean clues to the bigger mystery of who he was and who he was to become. He studied his fathers letters and absorbed what he could from his grandfather's circle of black friends, poker buddies, and drinking mates. But his father offered only vague aphorisms. "Like water finding its level,

"It was there [on the basketball court] that I would make my closest white friends, on turf where blackness couldn't be a disadvantage," Obama (going for the basket, left, and in his 1979 varsity team photo, far right, top row) wrote in *Dreams from My Father.*

"It's that fundamental belief— I am my brother's keeper, I am my sister's keeper—that makes this country work."

BARACK OBAMA

WE GO PLAY HOOP
Thanks Tut, Gramps, Choom Gang, and Ray for all the good times.
Barry Obama

you will arrive at a career that suits you," he wrote in one letter. And Gramps's pals were friendly enough, but as soon as the cards were dealt, they clammed up. Barry was left sitting at the bar of one of their hangouts in a Honolulu red-light district, "blowing bubbles into [his] drink and looking at the pornographic art on the walls."

From TV and radio and the movies he found some guidance, listening to Marvin Gaye croon and learning dance steps from *Soul Train*, watching the way Shaft walked and talked, and learning the joys of humor, language, and cursing from Richard Pryor. But he also noticed how Bill Cosby never got the girl on *I Spy* and how the black guy on *Mission: Impossible* never emerged from his subterranean lair into the light of day.

If his father's letters didn't help him find his way, the Christmas present he gave his son did. Unlike football, basketball was a game he was not bad at and that he played, he wrote, "with a consuming passion that would always exceed my limited talent." But he was talented enough to make his high school varsity team. And he played pickup games at the University of Hawaii, where black players taught him some of the rules of the other, bigger game: "That respect came from what you did and not who your daddy was"; that talking trash was fine, as long as you could back it up; and that a man should never show emotions, especially hurt and fear, that he didn't want an opponent to see.

Called "Barry"—the same name his father used in America—in high school, Obama used his grandmother's nickname ("Tut," or "Toot," is short for "tutu," "grandparent" in Hawaiian) in giving props to family and friends in his 1979 senior yearbook (left). Above, the moon shines over Diamond Head at dawn.

Years later he would realize, he wrote, that he "was living out a caricature of black male adolescence, itself a caricature of swaggering American manhood."

"Race is still a powerful force in this country, and there are certain stereotypes I will have to deal with. But I find that when people get to know you they will judge you on your merits."

BARACK OBAMA

Even so, on the basketball court he found a community of friends, white and black, among the latter his closest friend, Ray—an engaging, smart, and funny athlete, an Olympic-caliber sprinter whose potbelly made him not look the part. Ray was among a growing number of black kids who had moved to Hawaii from the mainland and whose "confusion and anger," Obama wrote, "would help to shape my own."

Bonding between themselves, Obama and Ray and their other black friends chuckled over the ways of "white folks," enumerating the slights and insults they'd endured. For his part, Obama recalled a seventh-grader who called him a "coon," a tennis pro who told him not to touch a posted tournament match schedule because his color would rub off on it, a basketball coach who complained that opponents in a pickup game were "a bunch of niggers."

At the same time, he felt removed from the easy camaraderie of his friends.

"Sometimes I would find myself talking to Ray about 'white folks' this and 'white folks' that," he wrote, "and I would suddenly remember my mother's smile, and the words that I spoke would seem awkward and false."

Obama in 1979 during his high school graduation in Hawaii with his maternal grandparents, Stanley Armour Dunham and his wife Madelyn Payne, both natives of Kansas (shown above). "His repeated acts of self-creation spoke to me," Obama wrote of Malcolm X (speaking at a Harlem rally in 1963, above) in his memoir. "The blunt poetry of his words, his unadorned insistence on respect, promised a new and uncompromising order."

Though Ray often told him how much he liked Gramps and Toot, his creeds about whites and their racist deeds caused Obama to remind him that "[They] weren't living in the Jim Crow south" or a "heatless housing project in Harlem or the Bronx. We were in goddamned Hawaii!"

And so his life became a routine of school and basketball, hanging out with his friends, and being home in time for dinner and to help Gramps do the dishes—slipping "back and forth between my black and white worlds."

But worlds collide, in small, inexplicable ways; he would flinch when a white girl said she liked Stevie Wonder or the lady at the checkout counter asked if he played basketball or the principal told him he was a cool dude. "I did like Stevie Wonder," he wrote, "I did love basketball, and I tried my best to be cool at all times." He tried to figure out why such seemingly innocent, offhand remarks riled him the way they did, but the answer eluded him.

In his search for role models and surrogates for the main character missing in his life, Obama found a trove in the books of James Baldwin, Ralph Ellison, Langston Hughes, Richard Wright, and W.E.B. DuBois. But even as he devoured them—reading not for entertainment as much as out of a hunger to discover their hidden meanings and deeply rooted truths—he was unsettled by what he found at their core. "I kept finding the same anguish," he wrote, "the same doubt; a self-contempt that neither irony nor intellect seemed able to deflect. Even Du Bois's learning and Baldwin's love and Langston's humor eventually succumbed to its corrosive force, each man finally forced to doubt art's redemptive power."

Only Malcolm X seemed not to have given up. Where the others withdrew ("exhausted, bitter men, the devil at their heels"), it seemed to Obama that Malcolm had invented his own path to redemption. But not even Malcolm could prescribe a treatment for his deepest pain, could not heal the wound of his rent worlds. "He spoke of a wish he'd once had, the wish that the white blood that ran through him, there by an act of violence"—rape—"might somehow be expunged."

For Obama, that would mean abandoning "the road to self-respect" that his search had put him on. He would be betraying himself, he wrote, if he "left my mother and my grandparents at some uncharted border."

"I have a number of political heroes, including iconic figures like Dr. King, Congressman John Lewis, and President Lincoln. These leaders are visionary, they are inspiring, and they gave those of us who watched or studied them a sense of hope and purpose and a reason to get involved."

BARACK OBAMA

Obama doesn't say so in his book, but during this period in his life when he was reading voraciously, educating himself, and plumbing the depths of his feelings, trying, however unsuccessfully at the time, to untangle and understand them, hoping to find the fully realized man—the father—in himself, the seed of a different kind of salvation began to germinate. He was beginning his education as a writer.

It would be decades before he would discover and realize his talent for the written word—he composed *Dreams from My Father* when he first began to practice law, in the early 1990s, long before his first forays into politics. But less than two years after he graduated from high school, he would discover the writer's most essential tool and his own greatest gift—his voice.

"Junkie. Pothead. That's where I'd been headed: the final, fatal role of the young would-be black man."

So Obama would describe himself as an eighteen-year-old freshman at Occidental College in Los Angeles, in 1979. "Pot had helped, and booze; maybe a little blow when you could afford it. Not smack though." He didn't try heroin, he wrote, because the guy who wanted to turn him on to it was shaking and sweating, and Obama didn't like the looks of the rubber tubing he tied off with and the needle he stuck in his arm. He wanted no part of the oblivion the man was pushing; it looked too much like death.

"If you feel good about me, there's a whole lot of young men out there who could be me if given the chance."

BARACK OBAMA

He did drugs in those days, not because he "was trying to prove what a down brother I was," he wrote, but because the high helped him "push questions of who I was out of my mind."

Occidental's was an idyllic, leafy campus near Pasadena and far from the sprawling ghettos on the south side of L.A. Obama was easily accepted into the black student population, many of them kids from the ghettos who were happy to have escaped the gritty and dangerous streets they'd grown up on. "I hadn't grown up in Compton, or Watts," Obama wrote. "I had nothing to escape from except my own inner doubt."

While Obama spent much of his time on Punahou's playfields (above) and received only "marginal report cards," he wrote, he devoured books by James Baldwin, Langston Hughes, Richard Wright, and other favorites that he found on the shelves of the school's library, located inside Cooke Hall (right).

COOKE HALL

"I am not opposed to all wars. I'm opposed to dumb wars."

BARACK OBAMA

Then there were the black kids from the suburbs, like one beautiful coed who got offended when Obama asked her if she was going to a Black Students' Association meeting. "I'm not black," she said. "I'm multiracial!"

Scornful as he was of those students' self-denial, he recognized part of himself in their "mixed-up hearts...Their confusion made me question my own racial credentials all over again."

Aligning himself with students whose black cred was unassailable, he made friends with one righteous dorm mate whose sister had been a founding member of a midwest Black Panther Party chapter and who himself had had run-ins with the police and had friends in jail. "His lineage was pure, his loyalties clear, and for that reason he always made me feel a little off-balance."

The strategy, to show that he was just as righteous as his dorm mate, backfired when,

Looking dapper in Mr. Eric Kusunoki's Punahou homeroom, Obama (left, standing center) first tested his writing talents on the staff of the school's literary journal, *Ka Wai Ola* ("The Living Water"). He posed (above) with his schoolmates for the yearbook in his senior year (second row, right).

to Obama's lingering shame, he mocked another friend, a black student, but one from a middle-class background who dressed like a preppy, "talked like Beaver Cleaver" and had a white girlfriend, for being a bogus brother.

"Why you say that, man?" said his dorm mate. "Seems to me we should be worrying about whether our own stuff's together instead of passing judgment on how other folks are supposed to act."

Later, the memory of that incident and the shame it induced, helped snap him out of his pot haze. It was his own fear of not belonging, he realized, that led him to ridicule his friend—the fear "that unless I dodged and hid and pretended to be something I wasn't I would forever remain an outsider, with the rest of the world, black and white, always standing in judgment."

He understood finally that he did not have to be slave to fear and anger and despair, that both worlds, black and white—his father's and mother's—were part of him. "Only a lack of imagination, a failure of nerve," he wrote, "had made me think that I had to choose" between them.

"Policy-by-slogan will no longer pass as an acceptable form of debate in this country."

BARACK OBAMA

A glimpse into the future occurred during his sophomore year, his last at Occidental, when, with the encouragement of a girlfriend, he became involved in the nationwide student movement to demand that colleges and universities divest themselves of financial interests that helped support the apartheid government of South Africa.

At a student rally, Obama rose to speak in public for the first time.

"There's a struggle going on," he said as students playing Frisbee on the campus common turned to listen along with a throng of students and professors. "It's happening an ocean away. But it's a struggle that touches each and every one of us...a struggle that demands we choose sides. Not between black and white. Not between rich and poor. No... It's a choice between dignity and servitude. Between fairness and injustice. Between commitment and indifference. A choice between right and wrong."

"Go on with it, Barack! Tell it like it is!" someone shouted.

But by prearrangement, he was dragged

off stage by two students dressed as soldiers, as an agitprop bit to dramatize the lack of free-speech rights in South Africa. As his friends pulled him away, however, he didn't want to give up the microphone. The audience was "clapping and cheering, and I knew that I had them, that the connection had been made…I really wanted to stay up there, to hear my voice bouncing off the crowd and returning back to me in applause. I had so much left to say."

Pauahi Hall is the centerpiece of Punahou's lush campus. During his years there—and later at Occidental College—Obama wrestled, he wrote, "in a fitful interior struggle" to find his identity as a man in the two vividly drawn—and fatherless—black and white worlds he was growing up in.

FINDING HIS WAY

During his time at Columbia University (right and top), where Obama transferred for his junior and senior years, he lived on a since-gentrified block on New York City's East Ninety-fourth Street (above).

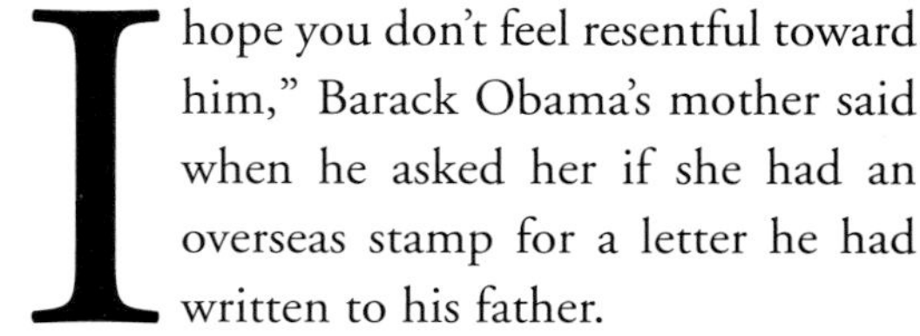

"I hope you don't feel resentful toward him," Barack Obama's mother said when he asked her if she had an overseas stamp for a letter he had written to his father.

He said, "No," but more than a decade had passed since he'd last seen him, and their correspondence had slowed to a trickle. He felt so estranged from his father in fact that he had started an earlier draft of the letter by writing "Dear Dr. Obama."

It was the summer between his junior and senior years at Columbia University and his mother and half sister Maya had come to visit him in New York, where he was working on a construction site and living in an apartment uptown at the edge of East Harlem that he shared with a Pakistani friend he'd known in Los Angeles.

He had transferred to Columbia determined to break out of the cocoon Occidental provided and the bad habits and self-indulgences he had found himself susceptible to there. He was also eager to escape L.A.'s suburban sprawl and live "in the heart of a true city," with black neighborhoods in close proximity.

Obama arrived in New York at the glitzy dawn of the go-go 1980s, when Wall

Street was booming and "Manhattan was humming" with new and more-expensive restaurants and nightclubs that catered to an exploding population of young urban professionals, "men and women barely out of their twenties [and] already enjoying ridiculous wealth."

Feeling the need to steel himself from temptation, Obama concentrated on his studies and resisted the invitation of his jovial, bar- and girl-crawling roommate's nightly forays. "You're becoming a bore," his roommate said. Obama, who ran three miles a day, fasted on Sundays and began keeping a journal in earnest (writing what he called "daily reflections and very bad poetry" but also passages that would become the source material for the memoir he would write a decade later), could not deny it was true.

When he wasn't attending classes or studying, he explored the city on foot and saw "beneath the hum" of the dazzling city the legions of unemployed and the abandoned, rat- and crack-infested tenements where the homeless took refuge and drug dealers preyed upon them. Little of the Reagan administration's touted "trickle down" economy seemed to be seeping far enough to thaw the permafreeze of poverty that trapped the have-nots in an underclass from which there seemed to be no escape.

"It was as if the middle ground had collapsed, utterly," he wrote, leaving rich and poor on opposite sides of the ever-widening maw between them. It was a racial as well as an economic gulf that threatened to become a cauldron, seething with hatred. Not even the hallowed halls of academia were immune from "the bile that flowed freely not just out on the streets but in the stalls of Columbia's bathrooms as well, where, no matter how many times the administration tried to paint them over, the walls remained scratched with blunt correspondence between niggers and kikes."

When his mother and sister visited in the summer of 1982, they found a young man far different from the disaffected slacker they would have encountered had they dropped by his dorm at Occidental three years before.

His mother was especially pleased to learn that he was writing to let his father know that he planned to visit Kenya after graduation the following summer. "I think it'll be wonderful for you two to finally get to know each other," she said and then went on to share her memories of his father, including one story about how he was an hour late for their first date. Waiting for him outside the university library, she'd fallen asleep on a bench. She woke to find her future husband standing over her with two friends. "You see, gentlemen," he said. "I told you that she was a fine girl, and that she would wait for me."

The way she told the story, smiling and laughing as she spoke, he saw the depth of her enduring love for his father. Even though he'd left her with a baby to raise on her own and she'd divorced him as a result, she loved him still. "She saw my father as everyone hopes at least one other person might see them," Obama wrote, adding that she had tried to make him, "the child who never knew him, see him in the same way."

Any hope of that happening appeared to end for good just a few months later when he received a telephone call from an aunt in Nairobi. His father had been killed in a car crash. He was forty-six years old. His son didn't shed a tear.

While his fellow Columbia graduates applied for high-paying corporate jobs or sent their applications off to grad schools, Obama felt fired by a passion instilled in him by stirring stories his mother told him as a boy about the civil rights movement and its brave freedom riders and heroic martyrs. He also had his own idealistic desire to give back to the community and to do what he could to help the powerless and disenfranchised free themselves from the cycle of poverty and despair.

Instead of mapping a path for a rapid ascent up the money ladder, he prepared for his graduation from Columbia in 1983 by writing letters to dozens of civil rights organizations, progressive politicians like Chicago's recently elected Harold Washington (the city's first black mayor), tenants' rights groups, and neighborhood associations all across the country.

When he heard back from a grand total of no one, he decided to bide his time, find a job, pay off his college loans, and try again. This time his job search was almost too successful. Hired by the multinational Business International Corporation as a research assistant, he was soon promoted to a higher-paying position as financial writer, with his own office, his own secretary, and money to burn, not to mention the admiration of the black women in the secretarial pool who took pride in him and predicted that one day he'd be running the company.

Obama was beginning to think he might like doing just that when he received another phone call from Africa, reminding him who he was. It was his half sister Auma calling to report another accident, another death. Another of his father's children—a boy named David, his half brother—had been killed in a motorcycle accident.

He wasn't sure why, but the news of the death of a stranger an ocean away who was also a brother reminded him that he had made a commitment to serve—or at least to become involved in something more important than an office on a higher floor with a better view. A few months later, he turned in his resignation and sent out another batch of letters looking for a job as a community organizer.

"There's nothing wrong with making money, but focusing your life solely on making a buck shows a poverty of ambition."

BARACK OBAMA

After six months, he got an offer to work as a trainee with a veteran grassroots organizer who was working to start job placement and training centers in neighborhoods on the South Side of Chicago that had been hard hit by plant closings and layoffs. The pay, $10,000 a year, with a $2,000 allowance to buy a car, would have been scoffed at by his friends. Even the security guard in his office building told him, "Forget about this organizing business and do something that's gonna make you some money...you can't help folks that ain't gonna make it no how, and they won't appreciate you trying." He took the job anyway.

Obama fell in love with Chicago as soon as he drove around it—cruising the shoreline drive along Lake Michigan and through the heart of the city the length of Martin Luther King Drive. He found the Regal Theater where Duke Ellington and Ella Fitzgerald used to perform. As he drove he recalled reading about Richard Wright delivering mail in Chicago while awaiting the publication of his first book. Obama communed with the

"Our individual salvation depends on collective salvation."

BARACK OBAMA

ghosts of the multitudes—those who made the great migration north from the Delta, seeking a better life and bringing their joyous and mournful, soul-stirring blues with them.

On his third day in town he happened into Smitty's Barbershop, a neighborhood place where the almost mythic warmth and easy conviviality made Obama feel instantly at home. He was just leaving when Smitty, the barber, told him he ought to "come back a little sooner next time. Your hair was looking awful raggedy when you walked in." Obama, who now lives with his wife and kids in nearby Hyde Park, has been coming back ever since.

If the intensive reading, journal-writing, and self-analysis Obama engaged in as a student provided the first foundations for his future career as a writer, the three years he spent in Chicago as a community organizer served as his political apprenticeship. And a demanding challenge it was, one fraught with frustration and infrequent rewards but one that taught him firsthand the plight of America's inner cities and the resilience of residents who feel at once powerless and hopeful that things can change.

He worked with a tiny network of community activists and volunteers from South Side churches who were attempting to help

residents improve conditions—and, often, simply cope—in deteriorating neighborhoods plagued by sky-high unemployment, crime, and high school dropout and teen-pregnancy rates. There were neighborhoods where city services, including police protection, were slow or faulty at best, where parks were left untended and schools underfunded,

Obama still lends a hand in the Chicago neighborhoods where he worked as a community organizer in the 1980s. Here he and Catherine Moore, a worker at the St. James Food Pantry, hand out Thanksgiving groceries in 2006.

where stores were closed and boarded up and where sometimes it seemed only those who couldn't afford to leave stayed. To get to know the community and its needs, Obama did the same thing he would do when he later ran for office: he knocked on doors and attended neighborhood meetings in church basements, school cafeterias, housing projects, lunch counters, barbershops, and street corners.

Two decades later when he announced his intentions to run for the presidency, Obama alluded to his years as a community organizer in Chicago. "I learned that meaningful change always begins at the grassroots," he said in a video statement to supporters, "and that engaged citizens working together can accomplish extraordinary things."

"You can't always come up with the optimal solution, but you can usually come up with a better solution."

BARACK OBAMA

Back in the mid-1980s, as he canvassed the neighborhoods of Chicago's South Side, he listened as people told him of their hardships and hopes and their anger. He and his group helped when they could, but often failed. When a woman he spoke with told him that a friend of her son's had been shot at in the street in front of his house, Obama met with other parents worried about increasing gang violence in their neighborhood and organized a meeting with a police district commander. The officer canceled. In his place a department public relations rep arrived and lectured the parents on the need to discipline their children.

It was at Chicago's Trinity United Church of Christ where Obama (attending a service there in 2004) heard the phrase "the audacity of hope" in a sermon delivered by his pastor, Rev. Jeremiah Wright Jr., on his first visit to the church two decades ago.

He had better luck with a campaign he spearheaded to get schools to adopt a counseling and mentoring program for at-risk teenagers. He also organized residents of South Side housing projects to demand that the city fulfill its asbestos-removal and job-training promises in the projects as effectively as in other, better-connected wards. Small neighborhood groups organized by Obama and his colleagues operated street cleanup campaigns and Crime Watch programs, successfully sought improved sanitation service from the city, and got the parks department to clean up and improve South Side green spaces and playgrounds.

His successes brought him some attention around town; he was invited to speak and join panels. "Local politicians knew my name," he wrote, "even if they still couldn't pronounce it."

Even so, the city's problems often seemed overwhelming. After three frequently frustrating years in Chicago, Obama realized he was tilting against the Windy City's entrenched, immovable power structure. As a street corner–church basement organizer he could work for twenty years and continue to run up against the same impediments—red tape, corruption, neighborhood leaders more interested in protecting their turf than improving it, and indifference. To effect real

change, he needed clout, the kind wielded by the lawyers and politicians who held the real power in the city. And so he applied to law school, "to learn power's currency in all its intricacy and detail," he wrote.

Before he left Chicago, promising to return after earning his law degree at Harvard, he attended a rousing service at the South Side's Trinity United Church of Christ. The full-throated congregation sang along with the gospel choir, their voices buoyed by organ surges as they swayed to a drummer's backbeat.

The sermon that Sunday, punctuated by shouts of "Say it!" and "Yessuh!" from the congregation, spoke to the myriad hardships—from overdue electric bills to marital abuse and failed schools—endured by those gathered there. The preacher, the Rev. Jeremiah Wright, identified the enemy common to all—despair—and its antidote, one without which no Freedom Rides would ever have been attempted, without which no artist would ever pick up a pen, no people would ever strive to create a better world. The sermon was called "The Audacity of Hope."

Obama never forgot it.

By the time he arrived in Kenya in 1987 for a monthlong visit prior to moving to Boston to begin law school, he had already learned some surprising truths about his father from his half sister Auma. During an earlier visit to Chicago, she had told Obama that she and her brother Roy were born before their father left for Hawaii in 1959. They were living with their mother in Kogelo when Barack, Sr. returned from America with a new wife, a white woman named Ruth. Auma and Roy went to live in Nairobi with their father—who was working for an American oil company—and Ruth, who eventually bore him two more children.

"The Old Man," as his African children called Obama's father, once owned a large house in Nairobi, drove a big car, and enjoyed high status and privileges thanks to friends in the highest reaches of the new government of independent Kenya. After he quit the oil company and joined the government, working in the Ministry of Tourism, however, he had a falling out with the president, Jomo Kenyatta, after tensions grew between Kenyatta's tribe—the Kikuyus, the largest in Kenya—and the Old Man's Luos.

Before long the Old Man was fired from his post and blacklisted; finding doors in all the ministries and government agencies closed to him, he ended up with an insignificant job in the Water Department.

Despondent over his reduced status and angry that his old friends treated him like a pariah, he began drinking heavily and frequently lost his temper with his wife and children. Ruth left him while he was recovering in the hospital for nearly a year after a car accident in which the other driver, a white farmer, had been killed. It was after he was released from the hospital that Obama's father visited Hawaii, to spend Christmas with his then-ten-year-old son.

Upon his return, he lost his job at the Water Department and had to move with his children into a dilapidated house in the slums of Nairobi.

By the time of his death, things had improved somewhat. He had returned to government following Kenyatta's death, working in the Ministry of Finance, and had even fathered another son. Yet despite flashes of his old charm, his last years, Auma said, were tinged with bitterness and regret.

For Obama, hearing this utterly unexpected accounting of his father's life, one that trampled all the myths that his mother and grandparents had woven for him, was unsettling to say the least. "I felt as if my world had been turned on its head; as if I had woken up to find a blue sun in the yellow sky; or heard animals speaking like men."

"What I want to be able to do if possible, and it's not always possible, is to engage people who disagree with me in a dialogue."

BARACK OBAMA

Auma took Obama to meet Dorsila, the youngest child of his great-great-grandfather

Obama learned more truths about his father's life from his step-grandmother (right) during his first visit to Kenya in 1987. Political differences with the nation's first president, Jomo Kenyatta, led Obama's father, Barack, to years of poverty and despair. Obama's older half brother Malik (below, in 2004), who lives in eastern Kenya, holds a photo of himself with his famous American brother and an unidentified friend.

Obama, who was in turn the great-great-great-great grandson of Owiny, the legendary Luo warrior whose armies defeated the Bantu nine generations before the white man came to Kisumu. Dorsilla was startled when Barack pulled out a Bic to light his cigarette.

"She wants to know where the fire comes from," Auma explained. "She says that things are changing so fast it makes her head spin. She says that the first time she saw television, she [thought] the people inside the box . . . were very rude, because when she spoke to them they never answered back."

It's only when you hitch yourself up to something bigger than yourself that you realize your true potential."

BARACK OBAMA

They were all sitting under a mango tree outside the house his father had built for his grandmother, one story, with crumbling concrete walls and a corrugated-tin roof, bougainvillea abloom all around, chickens pecking at the bare ground.

On a wall inside the house in Kogelo, a village about fifty miles north of the equator and near the shore of Lake Victoria—where just a few generations previously the clan existed as their people had for hundreds of years, living in a family compound, wearing nothing but goatskin loincloths, raising goats, and planting corn —hung his father's doctorate diploma from Harvard University.

Dorsila, who spoke only Luo, listened in nonetheless as Obama and Auma's "Granny" shared the oral history of their family.

"First there was Miwiru. It's not known who came before. Miwiru sired Sigoma, Sigoma sired Owiny . . ." She spoke in the cadence of Genesis, eventually tracing Mirwiru's descendants forward thirteen generations to the future United States Senator Obama. "When your grandfather was still a boy," she said, "we began to hear that the white man had come to Kisumu town. It was said that these white men had skin as soft as a child's, but that they rode on a ship that roared like thunder and had sticks that burst with fire."

Obama listened spellbound, much as his ancestors had when they gathered around the fire to listen to the wise elders or to itinerant harpist-poets who "sang of great deeds of the past."

But Granny's oral history was not of heroic deeds but of the wrenching change brought by the British, whose rule by gun and tax collector destroyed the Luo's ancient way of life in the span of a single generation. Obama's grandfather was among the first of his clan to adopt the white man's ways—trading his loincloth for suits and shoes, learning to speak, read, and write English—only to wind up embittered and broken after a lifetime of servitude to his colonial masters.

From Granny, Obama learned that the father who had abandoned him had been himself abandoned, at age nine, by his mother. As a teenager Barack, Sr. was beaten bloody and banished from home by his father for his rebellious spirit. Despite his stellar grades, Barack Sr. was expelled from a mission school. "He would sneak girls into his dormitory," Granny said, "for he could always talk very sweetly to girls." When he was arrested and jailed for his involvement in the independence movement, his father refused to bail him out. Barack Sr. was released soon after, but by twenty his dreams and ambitions to get the education he needed to create a better life had disappeared. He was married, with a son and a daughter—Auma—on the way, working at a menial job in Nairobi, and had no hope of ever achieving the bright future in an independent Kenya that he'd always imagined. Instead he would remain mired in poverty, stooped like his own father by despair and bitterness.

But then a chance meeting with two American educators living in Nairobi changed his life. They befriended him and, impressed by his bright mind and engaging manner, promised to help him get into a university if he completed a correspondence course for a secondary degree. Obama's father did as they suggested, passed the course, and proceeded to write dozens of letters to colleges and universities in America.

When Granny finished her story, she showed Obama copies of more than thirty letters, each with recommendations from his two American friends, that his father had written to schools in the United States and sent overseas.

Those letters were "like messages in a bottle," Obama thought later in reverie as he stood beside his father's unmarked grave at the rear of his grandmother's compound in Kogelo. "How lucky he must have felt when his ship came sailing in! He must have known, when that [acceptance] letter came from Hawaii, that he had been chosen after all; that he possessed the grace of his name, the *baraka*, the blessing of God."

As he stood there beside his father's grave, he felt that he knew and understood—and forgave—him for the first time in his life. His father had not succumbed to despair. He had had the audacity to hope.

And for the first time, his son wept for him.

POLITICAL APPRENTICESHIP

"Our party has chosen a man to lead us who embodies the best this country has to offer." Obama (top, and with Michelle, above) was talking about John Kerry at the 2004 Democratic Convention. He hopes the same will be said of him in 2008.

4

Waiting in the wings at the Fleet Center in Boston, where he was to give the keynote address at the 2004 Democratic Convention, Barack Obama had good reason to be nervous. And not just because he had been allotted seventeen minutes of uninterrupted prime time on all three broadcast networks and cable and satellite feeds that would carry his speech around the world.

The utterly obscure Illinois state senator had met John Kerry, his party's presidential standard-bearer, for the first time during the Illinois primary earlier that year when he spoke at a Kerry fundraiser. Obama was surprised and flattered a few weeks later when he received word that Kerry wanted him to speak at the convention. When Kerry's campaign manager called before the convention to tell Obama that he would be speaking not merely to state caucuses or to introduce one of the party's big guns to the delegates but delivering the keynote address, he was shocked.

And so was just about everyone else.

Democrats well remembered that in 1988, when another obscure politician

named Bill Clinton was tapped to deliver the keynote, the speech at the convention didn't go over any better than the party's candidate Michael Dukakis would in the general election that year.

Among the party faithful gathered at the Fleet Center, more than a few delegates surely were disappointed that some nobody from the midwest was going to address them rather than the likes of the Roosevelts and Kennedys of the party's glory years or, yes, Clinton, whose silver tongue had eventually carried them back into power four years after the Dukakis debacle.

Even David Axelrod, Obama's longtime friend and campaign manager, was "a nervous wreck" as zero hour approached. Obama tried to reassure him as the two arrived at the convention center. "I remember him patting me on the shoulder and saying 'Don't worry about it,'" Axelrod later recalled. "'I'll make my marks.'"

But alone in the green room with his wife, Michelle, an attorney who mentored him when he worked in the summer of 1988 at her firm after his first year in law school, he admitted he was feeling a bit queasy.

Obama recounts the moment in *The Audacity of Hope*: "She hugged me tight, looked into my eyes and said—'Just don't screw it up, buddy!'"

He didn't.

Wearing a borrowed tie, he stood on the dais and delivered a speech that Democrats—and many Republicans—hail as one of the greatest political convention keynotes in memory.

The convention hall rang with cheers as Obama spoke of the "true genius of America," a nation where "we can say what we think, write what we think, without hearing a sudden knock on the door...[where] we can participate in the political process without fear of retribution, and [know] that our votes will be counted—or at least, most of the time."

When he said that we live in a dangerous world where "war must be an option, but it should never be the first option," there was

"I'm a Democrat because we are the party that believes we're all in this together."

BARACK OBAMA

"We have an Administration that believes that the government's role is to protect the powerful from the powerless," Obama said (addressing the Democratic Convention, left, and campaigning for the Senate in Chicago in 2004, right and below).

no mistaking what he was talking about. He spoke about a young Marine bound for Iraq and eager to serve and perhaps die for his country. "I thought this young man was all any of us might hope for in a child. But then I asked myself: Are we serving [him] as well as he was serving us?"

And he stirred raw emotions when he spoke about the war's toll of soldiers killed—it was 900 then, more than 3,100 deaths ago—and maimed, returning home "with a limb missing or with nerves shattered."

A no-man-is-an-island theme ran through the speech: "If there's a child on the South Side of Chicago who can't read, that matters to me...If there's a senior citizen somewhere who can't pay for her prescription and has to choose between medicine and the rent, that makes my life poorer...If there's an Arab American family being rounded up without benefit of an attorney or due process, that threatens my civil liberties."

But it was his call for all citizens to come together in "a united American family" that many found most memorable: "[T]here's not a liberal America and a conservative America...There's not a black America and white America...there's the United States of America.

"The pundits like to slice-and-dice our country into Red States and Blue States... But I've got news for them...We worship an awesome God in the Blue States, and we don't like federal agents poking around our libraries in the Red States. We coach Little League in the Blue States and have gay friends in the Red States."

Closing with a plea that "out of this long political darkness a bright day will come," the speech was greeted by thunderous applause and ecstatic reviews for Obama's "mesmerizing" and "phenomenal" performance. *Time* rated it "one of the best speeches in convention history," and even the conservative *National Review* said the "simple and powerful" address was deserving of the "rapturous critical reception" it received.

In the aftermath of the torrent of praise and publicity, Obama would coast to victory in his own race for the U.S. Senate and score one of the few triumphs Democrats could cheer in an election in which they could not win the presidency and lost seats in both houses of Congress.

And so America's brightest new political star was born.

Wowing with his performance was nothing new for Obama. He first made national news in 1990 when he became the first black student elected president of Harvard Law School's prestigious *Law Review*. The resulting publicity brought calls from editors in New York who encouraged him to begin work on his memoirs, a heady proposition for a grad student not yet thirty years old.

His fellow students were impressed by his grace in the spotlight. "He didn't carry himself like the big man on campus that he clearly was," said Hill Harper, a former Harvard classmate-turned-actor (*CSI: New York*). And his constitutional law professor, Laurence Tribe—who would argue Al Gore's case against George W. Bush before the Supreme Court during the disputed election of 2000—chose him as his research assistant and later called Obama "one of

Obama posing in the office of *The Harvard Law Review* on February 5, 1999, after being named president.

the two most talented students I've had in thirty-seven years in teaching." (We're still waiting to learn the name of the other).

"After Harvard, Obama could have done anything he wanted," said David Axelrod. "He could have gone to the most opulent of law firms." Or, better yet for a graduating law student with lofty ambitions, a clerkship on the U.S. Court of Appeals, considered the fast track to clerking on the Supreme Court. But when appeals court Chief Justice Abner Mikva tried to hire him as his clerk, Obama said no thanks.

Before he graduated magna cum laude in 1991 Obama was being recruited by Wall Street firms and large corporate partnerships from across the country. When Chicago civil rights attorney Judd Miner read what turned out to be an erroneous report that Obama planned to join a silk-stocking firm

"Barack is the American dream . . . he is absolutely the best this country has to offer—and that makes the Democratic Party proud."

TERRY McAULIFFE, FORMER CHAIRMAN,
DEMOCRATIC NATIONAL COMMITTEE

in Chicago, he put in a call to the *Law Review*. The secretary who answered told him Obama wasn't in and asked if this was a recruiting call.

"I said 'I guess so,'" Miner recounted years later. "She said 'I'll put you on the list, you're number 643' or something like that."

Obama turned down the higher-paying jobs and to the delight of Miner and his partners took the position at the firm of Miner, Barnhill & Galland, where he worked on discrimination cases. "There aren't many blindingly talented people, and most of them are pains in the ass," one of the partners told *Time* after Obama left to run for the U.S. Senate. But "Barack," he added, "is the whole package."

Between cases, Obama worked on his memoir and in 1992, headed a statewide voter registration drive called Project VOTE that added 150,000 voters to the rolls and was credited with helping Bill Clinton carry Illinois in that year's election.

He also found time to teach constitutional law as a senior lecturer at the University of Chicago Law School, which he continued through January 2004, a full year after he began his race for the U.S. Senate. "Teaching keeps you sharp," Obama told the *New Yorker* that year. "The great thing about teaching constitutional law is that all the tough questions land in your lap: abortion, gay rights, affirmative action. And you need to be able to argue both sides. I have to be

able to argue the other side as well as [conservative Supreme Court Judge Antonin] Scalia does. I think that's good for one's politics."

In the summer after his first year at Harvard Law School (below left), Obama (receiving his diploma in 1991, above), began dating Michelle Robinson, an attorney in the Chicago corporate law office where he interned.

When Obama decided to try his hand at making law in addition to teaching it, he set his sights on an open Illinois state senate seat in a district that included both the university neighborhood of Hyde Park where he lived and some of the poorest neighborhoods in Chicago. Before launching his campaign however, he had to clear it with his wife, Michelle, herself a no-nonsense lawyer who looked dimly on politics.

"I said, 'I married you because you're cute and you're smart, but this is the dumbest thing you could have ever asked me to do,'" she later said in an interview. "Fortunately for all of us, Barack wasn't as cynical as I was."

Tall, bright, and gorgeous, Michelle, born in 1964, grew up half a continent and an ocean away from the homes in Indonesia and Honolulu where Obama grew up. "He had this mixed-up, international childhood, while I was Chicago all the way," Michelle, from a large family in a mostly black, blue-collar neighborhood on the South Side, told the *New Yorker* in 2004. "My grandmother lived five blocks away. Ozzie and Harriet, Barack called it," she said.

"I was just a typical South Side little black girl," she said. And one whose grades in school were good enough to get into Princeton University, where her older brother, Craig, was a star on the basketball team. "Of course it was different, being black," she told the *New Yorker*. "It was also different not being filthy rich."

After graduating cum laude from Princeton, Michelle also went to Harvard Law but didn't meet Obama until he arrived as a summer associate at the large corporate law firm where she worked in Chicago. Sharing Obama's discomfort in the boardrooms of high-end firms, she eventually left to start up a nonprofit leadership development program before going to work for the University of Chicago Hospitals, where she is now vice president for community relations.

They were married at the Trinity United Church of Christ, which they have attended ever since, in 1992 by Rev. Jeremiah A. Wright, the Chicago preacher whose "Audacity of Hope" sermon had so impressed Obama. Michelle's family and most of his, including his mother and half sisters Maya and Auma, attended the ceremony. "Our families get along great," Michelle told the *New Yorker*. After all, she pointed out, "we're both midwesterners. Underneath it all, he's very Kansas, because of his grandparents and his mom."

Obama with wife Michelle on their wedding day. His mother, Ann, who posed with Michelle's mom, Marian, at the couple's 1992 wedding (right), died three years later of cancer. *The Audacity of Hope* is dedicated to Obama's mother, "whose loving spirit sustains me still."

In 1996, after securing the support of his somewhat skeptical wife and encouragement from friends, colleagues at the university, and contacts he'd made as a civil rights lawyer, Obama, then thirty-five, ran for the Illinois legislature in the same South Side district where he had worked as a community activist and organizer a decade earlier. "I entered the race and proceeded to do what every first-time candidate does: I talked to anyone who would listen," he recalled in *The Audacity of Hope*. "I went to block club meetings and church socials, beauty shops and barbershops. If two guys were standing on a corner, I would cross the street to hand them campaign literature."

The tactics hadn't changed much since another Illinois lawyer, Abe Lincoln, first campaigned for office. They paid off for Obama, who won the race and arrived for the 1997 legislative session in Springfield, the state capital where Lincoln launched his political career and where Obama would formally announce his own presidential bid ten years later.

Like Washington in 2005, Springfield in 1996 had a minority Democrat assembly presided over by a Republican chief executive. "Democrats in Springfield," Obama wrote, "would shout and holler and fulminate, and then stand by helplessly as Republicans passed large corporate tax breaks, stuck it to labor, or slashed social services."

In a revealing scene in his book, Obama recalls a debate in which a Republican senator "worked himself into a lather" over a proposal to provide breakfasts to preschoolers because "it would crush their spirit of self-reliance.

"I had to point out," Obama writes, "that not too many five-year-olds I knew were self-reliant, but children who spent their formative years too hungry to learn could very well end up being charges of the state." The bill was defeated initially (a modified version later passed) and "Illinois preschoolers," he writes, "were temporarily saved from the debilitating effects of cereal and milk."

But needling opponents wasn't Obama's style when he joined the senate. Instead he worked with colleagues on both sides of the aisle, forged friendships over beers and bipartisan poker games—"I'm putting his kids through college," moaned one poker-playing Democrat—and won over just about everyone. "When he first came to Springfield, many resented his good looks, his articulate speaking ability, and his intellect," Republican state senator Kirk Dillard told *Washingtonian* magazine. But Obama impressed with his work ethic and commitment to getting things done. "He'll show up at any meeting that requires his attention," said Dillard. "If Barack has any enemies out there, they come from just sheer jealousy. I don't believe he has any enemies who have a good reason."

"Take a leap of faith with me."

BARACK OBAMA

we can!

"I knew from the day he walked into this chamber that he was destined for great things," another GOP senator told the *New Yorker*. "He's to the left of me on gun control, abortion. But he can really work with Republicans."

While not all his initiatives flew—one that he proposed in his first term to amend the state constitution to include health care as a right of all Illinois residents got nowhere—he successfully amended Republican tax-cut bills to include relief for low-income families. He skillfully worked a campaign-finance reform bill through the senate and got bills passed to expand early-childhood education programs and stop usurious lenders from charging sky-high mortgage rates to low-income would-be homeowners. "It's remarkable that a reform-minded newcomer could get as much accomplished as he did," Abner Mikva, the federal Court of Appeals judge who once tried to hire Obama, told *Washingtonian*. "He made a lot of friends."

During the first six of his eight years in the senate that he was in the minority party, Obama told *Harper's*, "I passed

"When people told me I couldn't win a Senate race in Illinois," said Obama (meeting with campaign aides, center; hands-free phoning in a hotel room, below right; and speaking at his Senate victory party, left, with Michelle and his daughters), "I didn't believe them."

"I think what people are most hungry for in politics right now is authenticity."

BARACK OBAMA

Grabbing a bite with Chicago mayor Richard Daley at Manny's Coffee Shop in 2004, Obama is now counting on the support of Daley and other Democratic allies in his run for the presidency.

"If you are a personal investment banker, you certainly want to invest in the Barack Obama IPO. . . . It is a solid investment in the American political scene."

SEN. DICK DURBIN

maybe ten bills...Most [were] in partnership with Republicans. The first year we were in the majority...I passed twenty-six bills in one year."

Many of those came out of the Health and Human Services Committee, which he chaired once the Democrats won control of the senate. But Obama's most innovative, controversial, and politically impressive success was his landmark 2003 bill to require police in Illinois to videotape interrogations in all capital crime cases.

Though convinced that capital punishment does not work as a deterrent, he does believe, he writes, that "there are some crimes—mass murder, the rape and murder of a child—so heinous, so beyond the pale, that the community is justified in expressing the full measure of its outrage by meting out the ultimate punishment."

At the same time, capital cases in Illinois at the time "were so rife with error, questionable police tactics, racial bias and shoddy lawyering" that thirteen wrongly convicted death row prisoners were exonerated and the governor was forced to order a moratorium on executions.

Despite the obvious need for reform, Obama began with virtually no support for his proposal—police and prosecutors were opposed, as were the newly elected Democratic governor and senators in both parties who feared being tagged soft on crime; even anti-death penalty groups were wary of reform rather than outright abolition.

Over a period of weeks, Obama convened meetings of all those groups who initially opposed the legislation. Rather than arguing the morality of the death penalty, Obama got everyone to agree on "the basic principle that no innocent person should end up on death row, and that no person guilty of a capital offense should go free." In the meetings Obama convinced police and prosecutors that videotaped interrogations would be a "powerful tool to convict the guilty," he later told *Time*, as well as save the innocent. Obama and his supporters agreed to modify the bill when police said parts of it would hinder investigations. But he refused their proposal that they videotape only confessions and not the entire interrogation because, he wrote, "the whole purpose of the bill was to give the public confidence that confessions were obtained free of coercion." In the end, the bill was passed unanimously and became law.

"A good compromise, a good piece of legislation, is like a good sentence. Or a good piece of music," Obama told the *New Yorker* the following year. "Everybody can recognize it. They say 'Huh. It works. It makes sense.' That doesn't happen too often [in politics], of course, but it happens."

After the thumping he received in 2000 when he lost the primary for Bobby Rush's congressional seat by a two-to-one margin, a Chicago pundit asked on TV: "Is Obama dead?"

And the following year, when a guerilla leader in Afghanistan sent squads of fanatic followers on a kamikaze mission to America, the pundit seemed to have the answer to his question. "The conventional wisdom," recalled David Axelrod, "was [that] no one named Barack Obama was going to get elected three years after 9/11."

Even so, when Republican U.S. senator Peter Fitzgerald announced he was retiring and another likely Democratic candidate Jesse Jackson Jr.—a popular Illinois congressman and a friend of Obama's (Jackson's sister Santita had been a bridesmaid at Barack and Michelle's wedding)—decided against it, Obama announced his candidacy in January 2003.

As he had when he first ran for office seven years before, he first made sure the admittedly "cockeyed idea" was okay with his wife, whom he calls one of the two "higher powers" that he consults before every major decision. Parents by then—daughter Malia was born in 1999 and her sister Sasha followed in 2001—the couple lived in a modest condo in Hyde Park, and though a two-income family, they weren't

DAWN

exactly rolling in money. Michelle knew the demands of campaigning, the amount of time her husband would be away, and the attention the girls wouldn't be getting from their father. Being a working mother and "the primary caregiver for two very bright little girls [is] crazy," she told the *New Yorker*. "It's not realistic."

She was also deeply skeptical of Obama's assurances that everything would work out. "I explained," he later told *Washingtonian*, "that what's going to happen is, I'm going to win the primary, win the general, and then I'm going to write a book."

"You are going to be a very credible presidential candidate."

ARCHBISHOP DESMOND TUTU TO OBAMA

As unlikely as that scenario must have sounded, she reluctantly agreed, but told him he "shouldn't necessarily count on her vote."

Or anyone else's for that matter. "Frankly," recalled Alabama congressman Artur Davis, "a lot of people believed that if you can't win a House seat, how are you going to win a Senate seat?"

Obama was facing a field of six other Democratic contenders, including the Illinois state comptroller, who had the backing of Chicago's legendary Democratic Party machine as well as the state's most powerful

"I have chosen a life with a ridiculous schedule," wrote Obama, whose long weekends at home allowed by his Senate schedule have become rarer during his presidential campaign. Here he pitches in with the breakfast dishes before getting Malia, left, and Sasha off to school one morning in 2006.

Obama walks with daughter Malia as she leaves their home in Hyde Park—a prosperous neighborhood on Chicago's South Side—on her way to school in October 2006 (left).

unions and a wealthy businessman with a $29 million campaign war chest. Obama had no real organization, just a small, untried staff of four working out of a tiny office in Chicago, few interested donors, and no support from the Democratic establishment.

When he traveled downstate, he drove alone in his own car and relied on the kindness of acquaintances and friends of friends to invite a few neighbors over for a chat around the kitchen table. When he could find enough people to fill a church basement or Rotary club, he would invariably explain that his father was from Kenya, in Africa, "which is where I got the name," and his mother was from Kansas, "which is why I talk the way I do."

When he marched in Chicago's St. Patrick's Day parade, a de rigueur rite for any Illinois politician, he and the army of ten volunteers he was able to muster brought up the rear, right in front of the garbage trucks.

Most observers assumed Obama would be swept from the campaign trail along with the rest of the paraders' trash. While he might win the vote in his district and other predominately black precincts around the state, few believed he could win votes in Chicago's suburban "collar" districts or in small towns downstate where, as a *New York* magazine writer put it—wittily but unfairly as it turned out—"the typical response to a person of color was to roll up the car windows."

But the smart money hadn't reckoned on Obama's appeal to voters in the suburbs and in the small towns and farmlands of central and south Illinois, where he campaigned vigorously, drawing handfuls of farmers and workers and shopkeepers and teachers to small coffee klatches at first, and before long, throngs. The overwhelmingly white suburbs weren't immune to Obama fever either. "Twenty years ago, if I'd said there would be lawn signs with pictures of an African American, with an African surname, all over my district on the Northwest side of Chicago, people would have had me tested for drugs," Rahm Emanuel, a former Clinton aide who is now a congressman from Illinois, told *New York*. "Yet there they were."

"Barack's got something different," said a downstate plumber. "He makes you feel like he's not a politician, but a leader."

"I know those people," Obama said as he drove through central Illinois with a writer from the *New Yorker*. "Those are my grandparents. The food they serve is the food my grandparents served when I was growing up. Their manners, their sensibility, their sense of right and wrong—it's all totally familiar to me."

Folks took to him in such numbers that he won the primary outright with 53 percent of the vote. But not before it was revealed that the ex-wife of the millionaire businessman who had been leading the field had sought a restraining order against him for striking her. Then came his general-election opponent, Jack Ryan, a conservative for whom the national Republican Party had high hopes of winning the seat—"Six-foot-four and Hollywood handsome…[Ryan] keeps in moral and physical trim by going to Mass and the gym each morning," enthused conservative columnist George Will.

White hope or not, Ryan was trailing Obama by sixteen points when, to make up lost ground, he hired conservative attack-specialist Scott Howell, famous for smearing Georgia senator Max Cleland, who had lost both legs in Vietnam, as unpatriotic and as dangerous to the nation's security as Osama bin Laden.

But Howell's tactics backfired when one of his operatives began stalking Obama with a video camera, following him everywhere and "standing less than two feet from Obama's face, barking questions," reported the Associated Press. Even Republicans were outraged. "Everybody knows politics is a contact sport," Obama said with aplomb. But he admitted he didn't like the intrusion, especially when the cameraman recorded him in private moments as he spoke to his wife and daughters on his cell phone. Obama turned the confrontations to his advantage however. "Scorched-earth politics," he called the tactic. "Precisely the kind of politics I want to change."

"I'm not sure anybody is ready to be president before they're president."

BARACK OBAMA

Ryan's campaign eventually unraveled altogether. He had to drop out of the race in the midst of the tabloid scandal that erupted when his ex-wife, *Boston Public* actress Jeri Ryan, alleged in divorce papers that Will's pious Republican hero had taken her to sex clubs and tried to get her to perform public sex with him.

In the wake of the flameout, desperate Republicans imported a replacement from Maryland, the rightist former presidential candidate Alan Keyes, apparently on the theory that only another black candidate

"Need just one ticket, willing to pay up to $75."

SIGN OBSERVED AT AN OBAMA RALLY

could challenge Obama. ("You know, me and you got something in common," George W. Bush would say when Obama met the president the following January. "We both had to debate Alan Keyes. That guy's a piece of work, isn't he?")

Indeed, Keyes's rants on the stump promptly alienated Illinois voters. "Saying that Jesus Christ wouldn't vote for Obama and that all gays are sinners," said one strategist, paraphrasing Keyes's typical talking points, "is beyond the bounds of acceptable speech in political debate."

If Keyes was foundering before Obama's keynote address at the convention, he stopped moving altogether afterwards. "I didn't realize that the speech would strike the chord that it did," Obama later told *Ebony*. "All I was really trying to do was describe what I was hearing on the campaign trail, the stories of the hopes, fears and struggles ordinary people are going through every day. People heard themselves in the speech and I think that made them respond."

After that it was all over but the voting. With Keyes's candidacy hopelessly behind and Obama's election virtually assured, he spent much of his time lending his newfound star power—and investing the political capital that came with it—by campaigning for other Democratic candidates around the country.

On election day he won in a landslide, with more than 70 percent of the vote and

scoring pluralities in every part of the state.

With the reissue of his memoir bound for the best-seller lists, he received a $1.9 million advance for three more books. With his financial worries over, he paid off his college loans and bought a $1.6 million home for his family in Hyde Park.

In January 2005, as he and his wife arrived at a hotel in Washington days before his swearing in as the junior senator from Illinois, Michelle remembered the prediction he had made at the beginning of the campaign when he told her his far-fetched plan to win the primary, then the election, and then write a book.

"We got off the elevator," he told *Washingtonian* magazine, "and she looked at me and said, 'I can't believe you pulled it off.'"

"I'd want to be a really great president, you know? . . . Because there are a lot of mediocre or poor presidents."

BARACK OBAMA

When his family was introduced to Vice President Dick Cheney following Obama's Senate swearing-in ceremony in January 2005 (above left), daughter Malia shook the veep's hand while Sasha slapped him five. "This is a new low in American politics," a newsman said of the aggressive tactics of Justin Warfel (with Obama, right), a Republican operative hired to videotape Obama's every move during the 2004 Senate race. His opponent apologized, and Obama (waiting to speak at an Illinois church later that year, above) continued his campaign unmolested.

MAN ON THE GO

As the new star in the Democratic ranks, Sen. Barack Obama was called upon by politicians across the nation to visit their constituencies and help win votes for the party in the crucial 2006 elections. The accommodating Obama crisscrossed the nation in a dazzling display of political support, in the process gaining increased recognition for himself that will be helpful in contests to come.

Clockwise from below: Obama in Missouri with Senate candidate Claire McCaskill; in Iowa with Sen. Tom Harkin; in Ohio with gubernatorial candidate Ted Strickland; in Los Angeles for gubernatorial candidate Phil Angelides; and in Bellevue, Washington, in support of Sen. Maria Cantwell.

HARKIN
U.S. SENATE
CALIFORNIA REPUBL

Clockwise from right: Obama signing books at a Philadelphia Democratic rally; in Florida with gubernatorial candidate Jim Davis; in Hoboken, New Jersey, supporting Sen. Bob Menendez; at a rally for Democratic candidates in Tempe, Arizona; in Little Rock, Arkansas, for gubernatorial candidate Mike Beebe; and in Nashville for Senate candidate Harold Ford Jr.

Bob Menendez
Democrat for NJ
Menendez2006.com
Bob Menendez
Bob Menendez
Bob Menendez
Democrat for NJ

SENATOR OBAMA

TAKES OFF

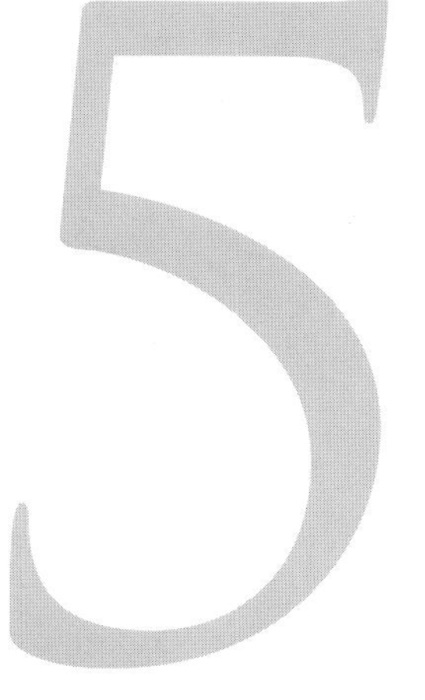

For more than twenty years, the U.S. Senate's two-man Illinois delegation hosted regular Thursday morning doughnuts-and-coffee get-togethers in the Capitol for Illinois residents who happened to be visiting Washington. The weekly Constituent Coffee meetings, a tradition begun by Illinois's popular late former senator Paul

As a member of the newly Democratic-controlled Senate Foreign Relations Committee, Obama, who takes the subway (left) to travel from his office (center) to committee meetings (right), concentrated on world affairs during his first two years in office.

Senator Obama, at work in his Chicago office, October 2, 2006.

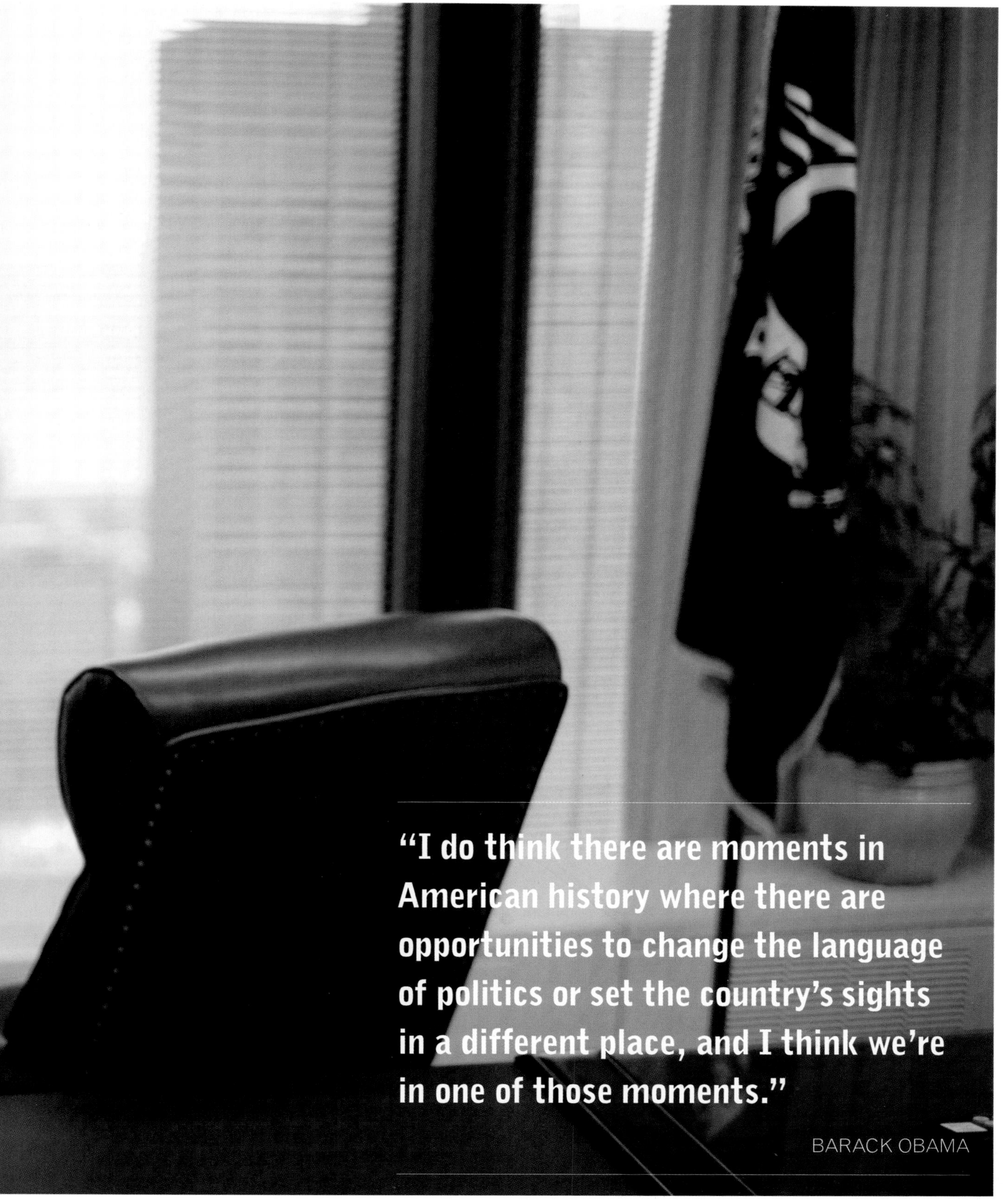

"I do think there are moments in American history where there are opportunities to change the language of politics or set the country's sights in a different place, and I think we're in one of those moments."

BARACK OBAMA

Simon in 1985, gave regular folks a chance for an informal give-and-take with their elected officials and provided a setting for the senators to keep in touch with the voters back home.

The coffee meetings were always friendly but subdued gatherings of seldom more than a few dozen people. That all changed when Barack Obama arrived in the Capitol to more hoopla than any freshman senator in memory save Bobby Kennedy and Hillary Clinton. The Thursday coffee klatches had to be moved to a larger room in order to hold the none-the-less-overflow crowds of Obama fans, not all of them from Illinois.

"America is ready to turn the page. America is ready for a new set of challenges. This is our time. A new generation is ready to lead."

BARACK OBAMA

It looked like Obama and Illinois's senior senator, Dick Durbin, would have to start holding the meet-and-greets in stadiums to accommodate the staff, security, and media entourage who traveled in Obama's wake after he announced his presidential candidacy. Even before then, the coffees—lively sessions in which Obama and Durbin responded to questions from constituents—had begun to seem less like informal chats around the breakfast table and more like full-blown events where as many as one hundred and fifty people would fill the chairs, while dozens more stood in the back of the room and more still were turned away at the door. At one 2006 meeting, when Obama introduced Durbin as one of *Time* magazine's ten best senators, Durbin deferred to his younger colleague's star power, saying, "I haven't done the cover of *Newsweek* or won a Grammy."

At another Thursday coffee, Durbin reminded the crowd that after Obama threw out the first pitch at a Chicago White Sox game the previous year, the Sox went on to win the World Series for the first time in eighty-eight years. When an Illinois college student asked if he could do the same for the even-more-woeful Cubs, who marked the one-hundredth anniversary of their last championship season in 2007, Obama said, "My arm is only so good."

Many Democrats, whose memory of their party leader's last White House residence has begun to feel almost as distant, held high hopes that Obama could work his magic for them, if not for the Cubbies.

After his swearing-in to the Senate on a bright and warm winter day in January 2005, with his wife and children and family members from Hawaii and Kenya proudly looking on, Obama attended a reception in the East Room of the White House. As he walked through the crowd of mostly Republican congressional newcomers, a photographer asked a reporter standing nearby, "Who is that guy?" Without waiting for an answer, he added, "He's certainly got 'It.'"

"The Natural," *The Atlantic Monthly* called him a little less than two years later, following the 2006 midterm elections when Obama's stumping for Democrats helped sweep them back into power and he was

Suave southpaw Obama twirled the first pitch in a White Sox playoffs game in 2005, his home team's championship season (above), chatted in the halls of the Senate chamber (top right), and looked in A-OK form during a 2006 staff meeeting (right).

hailed as the bright, vigorous, young star of the newly resurgent party. "Obama has already established himself as the paramount leader of the next generation," declared one Democratic power broker. "There's no one even close."

Britain's *New Statesman* called him one of ten people "who could change the world." The online magazine *Slate* dropped the qualifier: Obama already had "turned American politics upside down."

"If you were my husband, I wouldn't let you go around alone."

FEMALE GUEST AT A ILLINOIS DENTAL SOCIETY DINNER TO OBAMA

The site's editor, Jacob Weisberg, was speaking with urgency about an event then still two years in the future—the 2008 presidential elections. A short while before, New York senator Hillary Clinton, who hadn't yet declared her candidacy for her party's nomination, was nonetheless widely regarded as the Democrat to beat. Not so fast, said Weisberg. Obama, he wrote, "not Hillary [would] be the de facto Democratic front-runner" should he join the race.

When, in December 2006, Obama confessed that he was considering just such a course, the possibility of his candidacy became the talk of the republic. Oprah, Larry King, and Jay Leno lined up to get him to announce on their shows. "If Obama runs, he wins," posted Markos Moulitsas of the liberal blog *Daily Kos*.

When Charlie Rose asked guest Nora Ephron—a Washington insider once married to *Washington Post* journalist Carl Bernstein—who was on air to plug her book *I Feel Bad About My Neck* if she thought Obama was ready for the job, Ephron made it clear she liked him better than she liked her own body parts. "I don't want to wait until he is ready," said the screenwriter whose films *Sleepless in Seattle* and *When Harry Met Sally*...demonstrated her acute sense of the zeitgeist. "I'm ready for Barack Obama. I don't think we have six years to

A persuasive speaker, Obama (meeting with a student group in 2006) disarmed a skeptical audience during a speech on Israel. "[H]e was incredibly thoughtful," said one audience member. "And the crowd was just wowed. Barack managed to make those people who disagreed with him feel comfortable with the disagreement."

"If there's a child on the South Side of Chicago that can't read, that makes a difference in my life, even if it's not my child."

BARACK OBAMA

wait for him, because things are going to hell in a handbasket."

Democrats weren't alone in seeing Obama as a formidable candidate. "In Republican circles," said a former fellow Illinois state senator, "we've always feared that Barack would become a rock star of American politics."

"Barack Obama is a walking, talking hope machine," said Texas Republican Mark McKinnon, who has worked as an aide to George W. Bush. "People see him as a reflection about what is good and great about America. He's like a mirror of what people think we ought to be. He is successful, talented, respectful, moderate, judicious, thoughtful, and deeply human."

McKinnon went so far as to coin a

Three presidents? Obama flew to Houston following Hurricane Katrina with Bill Clinton and George H. W. Bush to speak with displaced New Orleans residents in September 2005. In the Senate, he cosponsored a bill to stop the second Bush administration from awarding no-bid reconstruction contracts.

potential Obama slogan. "I think people see him as a human bridge that can unite the country," he wrote in an e-mail to a reporter, dubbing the possible President Obama the "healer-in-chief."

Even Bush's Director of Strategic Initiatives, Peter Wehner, applauded the senator-author's call to stop all the bitter bickering and come together to get things done for the good of the country: "Barack Obama comes across as reasonable, civil, above-the-fray, well intentioned, fair-minded, non-ideological, agreeable."

Obama earned those kind of kudos from the opposite side in his first two years in the Republican-controlled Senate, just as he did as a progressive, minority-party state senator in Springfield. "If Barack disagrees with you or thinks you haven't done something appropriate," said Oklahoma's Tom Coburn, one of the most conservative Republicans in the Senate, "he's the kind of guy who'll talk to you about it. He'll come up and reconcile: 'I don't think you were truthful about my bill.' I've seen him do that. On the Senate floor."

Coburn and Obama struck up a friendship when they both arrived in Washington in 2005 as incoming senators. The two socialized, had brainstorming sessions during informal dinners, and cosponsored a number of bills, including one that passed in both houses of Congress to create a public Internet site that enables taxpayers to track how the government spends their money. They also joined forces in the wake of Hurricane Katrina to stop the Bush administration from funneling taxpayer money to hand-picked companies by awarding no-bid contracts for reconstruction projects in the ravaged Gulf Coast.

"I am just very impressed with him as a man, as a lawyer, as an individual, and as someone who chose not to go to a law firm but to be a community organizer and to do something about community problems."

VERNON JORDAN, OBAMA FRIEND AND CLINTON ADMINISTRATION ADVISOR

At least some of Obama's bipartisan appeal, noted *The Nation*, stemmed from the realization of Republicans that Obama's star power would enhance any bill he cosponsors with them. But Coburn said that Obama transcends party lines in a way that a true statesman should.

"What Washington does," Coburn said in *Harper's*, sounding very much like he had read *The Audacity of Hope*, "is cause everybody to concentrate on where they disagree as opposed to where they agree. But leadership changes that. And Barack's got the capability, I believe—and the pizzazz and the charisma—to be a leader of America, not [just] a leader of Democrats."

Baseball was one subject George W. Bush and Obama (with Sen. Dick Durbin, left, and White Sox owner Jerry Reinsdorf, right, following a salute to the 2005 World Series winners) saw eye to eye on.

There were plenty of Democrats who believed Obama has what it takes to lead the party straight back to the White House. Former Senate Minority Leader Tom Daschle, now a political consultant in Washington, said he sees Obama as a rising star the Democrats might do well

to attach their aspirations to. "He has got as much [charisma] as anybody I know." Daschle said, "Obama is the real thing. He has grown in stature in so many different ways in the short time that he has appeared on the public scene. He's a rising star, like a lot of people in other walks of life. We call them 'overnight sensations.' But he worked to get to this point. There is nothing 'overnight' about Barack Obama."

Other Democrats were almost giddy in anticipation of him running. Calling him "the first post-ideological candidate," Rahm Emanuel, the Illinois congressman and powerful Democratic national strategist, said he thinks "Barack could be a player in all fifty states...There are states we have lost, historically, that he'd be a major player in."

For out-of-power Democrats, particularly progressives who had all but given up on the social, economic, and foreign policy reforms they long for, Obama's appeal is almost intoxicating. "When you do political stuff and you run into a Barack," said Judd Miner, the civil rights attorney who recruited Obama to join his law firm in 1991, "you think, 'Oh, there's hope!'"

A similar kind of recognition inspires the armies of activist volunteers that Obama has attracted to his presidential campaign. "People call it drinking the juice," said Dan Shomon, who, as political director of Obama's Senate campaign, helped marshall his candidate's eager supporters to canvas neighborhoods, distribute literature, work phone banks, and drive voters to the polls. "People start drinking the Obama juice [and] you can't find enough for them to do."

"We must understand that the might of our military has to be matched by the strength of our diplomacy."

BARACK OBAMA

But some Democrats wondered if the Obama high is good for the party. Where there are many who compare Obama to successful charismatic candidates of the past ("He awakens that JFK appeal of a candidate who is young, attractive, and brainy," said Princeton presidential scholar Fred Greenstein) others said Kennedy's war service and experience made him more qualified than Obama. Kennedy won Navy and Marine Corps medals for heroism in the Pacific and was twice elected to the Senate and served eight years before entering the White House

> **"War hero against snot-nosed rookie."**
>
> BARACK OBAMA, ON A POSSIBLE SOUNDBITE FOR A McCAIN-OBAMA PRESIDENTIAL RACE

in 1961. Obama, critics noted, has gone through the fire of only a single Senate race and will have served only four years by 2009, when the next administration begins.

Supporters point out that Obama will be forty-seven by then (JFK was only forty-three when he was inaugurated) and that his critics discount the seven years he spent in the Illinois legislature. And, they add, the current president served a single term as governor in a state where the legislature has more power than the executive branch and prepared for political office by running a failed oil-drilling company and serving as partial owner of a baseball team. Obama by contrast, toiled for years helping the poor and disenfranchised as a community organizer and civil rights attorney.

"The important thing is not experience per se—Donald Rumsfeld and Dick Cheney had the best résumés in Washington and initiated a fiasco in Iraq," Obama said last year, "but rather, does someone have the judgment necessary to learn from experience and make good decisions?"

"It's not experience that people are demanding," Republican pollster Frank Luntz told the *National Journal.* "It's capability. It's not 'have you done it before?' It's 'could you do it in the future?' And Obama has that 'could-do-it' image."

"People want confidence that a president will lead and have strong convictions and integrity," added former Bill Clinton Press Secretary Mike McCurry. "Senator Obama exudes all that out of every pore."

Other critics questioned Obama's electability in the Democratic primary, much less the general election against as formidable an opponent as the then Republican front-runner John McCain, the four-term senator and decorated former Vietnam POW whose medals in a time of war—even one as unpopular as the disastrous one in Iraq—would shine all the more.

Supporters said Obama's comparative youth will work in his favor. He's twenty-five years younger than McCain and thirteen years younger than Hillary Clinton. "There's something to be said," Jennifer Senior wrote in a good-humored and insightful article in *New York* about Obama's post–baby boomer appeal, "for a politician who didn't come of age wearing sideburns and listening to Simon and Garfunkel."

Obama himself sees his youth as an advantage with an electorate that, he told Senior, has tired of leaders arguing over old issues. "These are fights that were taking place back in dorm rooms in the sixties," he said, alluding to so-called culture war squabbles over issues like Vietnam and sexual freedom.

"I think people feel like, 'Okay, let's not re-litigate the sixties forty years later.'"

Even an Obama critic like *New York*'s John Heilemann agreed: "The essence of Obama's pitch is that it's time to move past the old politics and that he's the embodiment of the new. And after the scorched-earth tactics and wretched polarization of the Clinton-Bush years, anyone who dismisses the potency of that message hasn't been paying attention."

Well before the primary season began, Hieleman pointed out that much of the early enthusiasm for Obama was based on the notion that he is simply not Hillary Clinton, whom many then regarded as the strongest candidate to win the Democratic nomination, but who, as a writer in the *National Journal* put it, would be "likely cannon fodder in the general election." As a political strategist told the magazine: "There's great fear in Democratic circles that...in the general election [Senator Clinton] cannot win. The thirst for a new face is palpable. I hear it in almost every political conversation with a Democrat."

Combining business and pleasure, Obama met with Archbishop Desmond Tutu during a fact-finding visit to South Africa and Kenya, where he spoke on the AIDS and Darfur crises and scolded the Kenyan government for human-rights abuses and restricting civil rights in a nationally televised speech in August 2006.

At the same time, Heilemann wrote, "What Obama has going for him that Hillary does not is that people genuinely like him. The power of personality in politics cannot be overstated." Even so, he added, "Hillary Clinton remains the prohibitive favorite to win the Democratic nomination. She has the money. She has the résumé. She has the policy chops, the shrewdest political adviser on the planet (i.e., her husband), and the unwavering allegiance of a substantial bloc of her party's primary voters."

"He may not have forty years in politics, but he's not exactly a child here. He's a well-established guy who knows a lot about the world."

WILLIAM M. DALEY, FORMER U.S. SECRETARY OF COMMERCE, ON OBAMA

And Heilemann was also among those who said Obama could wither in the heat of the general-election campaign. As a Democratic strategist in that camp said of Obama, "He's never been tested, never been scrutinized. There's never been anyone who's pored through his past the way the Republicans will. He would be a stronger candidate if he had gone through that crucible of fire."

Obama agreed as much, telling a reporter that because his Republican opponent dropped out of the race before his newly hired attack specialist could formulate an effective strategy, "I sort of got a free pass ...I wasn't subjected to a bunch of negative ads. And nobody thought I was going to win. So I basically got into the habit of pretty much saying what I thought. And it worked for me. So I figured I might as well keep on doing it."

But in anticipation of just such attacks, his own campaign pored over his state senate record to find the kind of information the Republicans might use against him. His researchers, he writes in *Audacity*, "didn't find a lot, but they found enough to do the trick—a dozen or so votes that, if described without context, could be made to sound pretty scary."

One was a drug-crimes bill "so poorly drafted that I concluded it was both ineffective and unconstitutional." Obama voted against it, leaving him open to an attack ad like one his research staff suggested the Republicans might use: "Obama voted to weaken penalties on gang-bangers who deal drugs in schools." Another claimed he had voted against a bill to "protect our children from sex offenders." Obama protested that he pressed the nay rather than the aye button by mistake and had the vote quickly corrected in the official record. "Somehow I don't think that portion of the official record will make it into a Republican ad," his campaign manager, David Axelrod, said with a wry smile.

As for his short tenure in the U.S. Senate, Obama was well aware going into the primaries that Democrats as well as Republicans were already looking through his voting record for mud to sling. Most political analysts agree that one of the reasons only two sitting senators—Warren G. Harding and John F. Kennedy—have ever been elected president since 1900 is that their voting

The day after Obama and his wife took AIDS tests (right) in Kisumu, Kenya, to dispel local fears that have slowed progress in fighting the disease, he posed with a high-minded observer near the Somalia border in August 2005.

LIFE

"In a country of 300 million people," Obama told an interviewer in his Senate office after the 2006 midterm elections, "there is a certain degree of audacity required for anybody to say I'm the best person to lead this country."

records provide much fertile ground for such searches.

In a wonderfully anecdotal and insightful chapter in his book about the history and inner workings of the Senate, Obama quotes a passage from Kennedy's *Profiles in Courage* about "the dread finality of decision that confronts a senator facing an important call of the roll.

"He may want more time for his decision," Kennedy wrote, "he may believe there is something to be said for both sides—he may feel that a slight amendment could remove all difficulties—but when that roll is called he cannot hide, he cannot equivocate, he cannot delay."

Ranked ninety-ninth in seniority in the one-hundred-seat Senate, Obama was careful during his freshman year to not allow his star power to intrude on the chamber. "He doesn't want to be this messianic figure carrying stone tablets," Axelrod told a reporter. "He understands he has to do the work." Said Michelle Obama: "I see my husband rolling up his sleeves and finally doing something to warrant all of this attention."

For Obama, getting down to work meant politely turning down some three hundred invitations per week to speak or appear on talk shows and at public events. Instead he kept a low profile and concentrated on hiring staff (including Daschle's former chief of staff), making friends on both sides of the aisle, and conferring with elders like Ted Kennedy, Robert C. Byrd—the ninetyish long-ago member of the Raleigh County (West Virginia) Ku Klux Klan, with whom he formed a close bond—and, yes, Hillary Clinton. He also focused on nuts-and-bolts issues like veterans' disability and federal infrastructure spending, which were of concern to the folks back home, and bills scheduled to come up for any of JFK's unforgiving roll calls.

Just two weeks into his term, one of those roll-call votes put him on the outs with his own party and some of his biggest campaign contributors. Obama voted with Republicans on a bill to limit class-action lawsuits, alienating the consumer, labor, and civil rights groups that supported him, not to mention lawyer groups that had contributed heavily to his campaign. "When multimillion-dollar settlements are handed down and all the victims get are coupons for a free product, justice is not being served," Obama, who believes such suits should be heard in state or federal—not local—courts, said in a statement explaining

"Our leaders in Washington seem incapable of working together in a practical, common-sense way. Politics has become so bitter and partisan, so gummed up by money and influence, that we can't tackle the big problems that demand solutions."

BARACK OBAMA

his vote. "And when cases are tried in counties only because it's known that those judges will award big payoffs, you get quick settlements without ever finding out who's right and who's wrong."

"Are you going to try to be president? Shouldn't you be vice president first?"

MALIA OBAMA, POSING A QUESTION TO HER FATHER

Todd Smith, the president of the Association of Trial Lawyers of America, one of Obama's contributors and a major force behind the bill he voted against, visited him to express his disappointment. The lobbyist told *American Prospect* magazine that his group's political action committee would continue to contribute to Obama's campaigns. "It was quite open," Smith said. "He said, 'Todd, go right ahead, speak your mind.' And I did. He believed there needed to be changes and...he felt [his vote] was the right way to go. I don't think your support for somebody rises or falls on a single issue. He will be there for regular people and their rights the vast majority of the time, and when he's not, it's going to be—at least in his mind, I'm certain—for solid reasons. He's an outstanding U.S. senator already."

"It's very difficult to think about something as massive as running for president at this time," Michelle (with her family in Hyde Park, above) said in March 2006. "That is not a part of our day-to-day conversation." Apparently it was by December, when Obama spoke in New Hampshire, a month before he launched his campaign for the White House (right).

While he sided with his party in most votes, including those on Bush's Supreme Court nominees (he voted nay), stem-cell research (aye), and an amendment to the constitution to outlaw flag-burning (nay), he angered party liberals by modifying his previously strong antiwar position after repeated visits to the country on fact-finding trips during his first two years in office.

"Hillary Clinton can't match Obama's rhetorical skills and often doesn't come across well in larger groups," wrote one commentator about Obama (with Clinton at the 2006 NAACP convention, below; and campaigning for Illinois Iraq war veteran Tammy Duckworth, right). "She wins over smaller groups and individuals one-on-one. Obama is the master of the large group."

He still thinks the invasion of Iraq was a disastrous mistake, opposes Bush's "surge" in troop levels, and calls for an immediate redeployment to prevent American soldiers from being caught in the cross fire of a bloody sectarian civil war. However in 2006 when Democratic congressman John Murtha called for immediate withdrawal, Obama spoke to the Chicago Council on Foreign Relations, saying among other things that the United States must "manage

"I personally have high hopes for him."

HAROLD M. ICKES, HILLARY CLINTON SENATE CAMPAIGN ADVISOR, ON OBAMA

our exit in a responsible way—with the hope of leaving a stable foundation for the future."

Washington Post columnist David Broder praised Obama for finding a "sensible common ground" and pointing "the administration and the country toward a realistic and modestly hopeful course on Iraq."

From the beginning of his campaign, Obama tried to take a fresh look at old conundrums that the Democrats have long wrestled with. "Sometimes," he said of the Republican lock on votes from the Christian Right, "the Democratic Party, I think, just assumes that as long as people are in church that somehow we can't reach them, that we have nothing in common. That's simply not true and certainly hasn't been true historically." And as for the Christian Coalition and other politically active religious groups, he said "religious folks need to understand that separation of church and state isn't there just to protect the state from religion, but religion from the state."

When he appealed to union groups to accept globalization as a fact of life during his Senate campaign, *New Yorker* writer William Finnegan asked him if he wasn't, "waving a red flag in front of labor."

Obama replied: "Look, those guys are all wearing Nike shoes and buying Pioneer stereos. They don't want the borders closed. They just don't want their communities destroyed."

On universal health care, Obama said that Democrats had not pushed hard enough for fear of being attacked as "'tax-and-spend liberals.' But that's not a good reason to not do something," he said. "You don't give up on the goal of universal health care because you don't want to be tagged as a liberal. People need universal health care."

"To me," he told one reporter, "the issue is not, 'Are you centrist or are you liberal?' The issue to me is, 'Is what you're proposing going to work? Can you build a working coalition to make the lives of people better?' And if it can work, you should support it whether it's centrist, conservative, or liberal."

In another interview, Obama described himself as a politician whose "values are deeply rooted in the progressive tradition, the values of equal opportunity, civil rights, fighting for working families, a foreign policy that is mindful of human rights, a strong belief in civil liberties, wanting to

"There's an optimism and lack of anger," New Jersey governor Jon Corzine said of Obama (carrying Thanksgiving groceries for a food-bank client, below; and visiting Nelson Mandela's former jail cell in Cape Town in 2006, right). "There is a reach for a positive framing of even negative issues."

"One thing I'm convinced of is that people want something new."

BARACK OBAMA

Sharp ears to go with the silver tongue: As he did at a forum in Boston (above), Obama listened carefully at a meeting of Illinois nuclear weapons plant workers (right, in 2006) and then spoke for their cause before the Federal Advisory Board on Radiation and Worker Health.

be a good steward for the environment, a sense that the government has an important role to play, that opportunity is open to all people, and that the powerful don't trample on the less powerful."

As for his ability to convey his vision to the electorate, Obama said he had no doubt. "I feel confident that if you put me in a room with anybody—black, white, Hispanic, Republican, Democrat—give me half an hour and I will walk out with the votes of most of the folks," he told *Newsweek.* "I don't feel constrained by race, geography, or background in terms of making a connection with people."

Maintaining that connection is one of the things Obama said he loves most about politics. He hosted more than forty town meetings in Illinois after his term in Washington began. In the sessions, convened in high schools, on college campuses, or in libraries in towns and cities across the state, Obama took questions and, he wrote in *Audacity,* "I answer to the people who sent me to Washington...They ask me about prescription drugs, the deficit, human rights in Myanmar, ethanol, bird flu, school funding, and the space program...And as I look out over the crowd, I somehow feel encouraged. In their bearing I see hard work. In the way they handle their children I see hope. My time with them is like a dip in a cool stream. I feel cleansed afterward, glad for the work I have chosen."

The thing Obama said he liked least about Washington was that it's not home—not yet anyway. During Senate sessions he arranged his schedule so that he could fly back to Chicago on Thursday nights, spend the weekend with his family and return to Washington on Mondays. Obama did his best to help Michelle around the house, pitching in to see that their daughters, Malia and Sasha, get to school and home in time for piano and ballet classes and homework.

Michelle, who runs the University of Chicago Hospitals' ambitious community relations and diversity programs, as well as the Obama household, was dubbed "the quintessential working Sister" by *Ebony* magazine. But the lot of the political wife "is hard," Michelle told the *New Yorker's* William Finigan. "And that's why Barack is such a grateful man."

When Obama was elected to the Senate, he and Michelle agreed that she and the children would remain in Chicago where she has a large support group, with her mother and brother (her father died before she and Obama married), relations and friends all living nearby. "I have a big village here," Michelle told *Ebony*. "Unless it was

"We need to take faith seriously—not simply to block the religious right, but to engage all persons of faith in the larger project of American renewal."

BARACK OBAMA

"The Land of Lincoln Loves Senator Obama."

SIGN OBSERVED AT AN ILLINOIS AFL-CIO MEETING

"Obama!" George W. Bush said at a 2005 White House reception the day before his swearing-in to the Senate. "Come and meet Laura. Laura, you remember Obama. We saw him on TV during election night." Obama (at the White House, above; getting the kids to school in Chicago, right; and on the road, inset) recounts the scene in his book: After shaking hands, "The president turned to an aide nearby, who squirted a big dollop of hand sanitizer in the president's hand." At upper right Michelle speaks to a high school economics class in Elmhurst, Illinois.

absolutely necessary, we felt it would just be good to stay close to our base. It's proven to be a smart move, and [Barack's] come to understand the wisdom of my plan."

Whenever Obama arrives home from Washington or the campaign trail, he has to check his superstardom at the door. "Giving a good speech doesn't make you Superman," Michelle told a reporter following his 2004 Democratic Convention keynote address. And she has never been shy about pointing out to reporters that he stays up late, doesn't make his bed, and leaves dirty socks on the floor.

When Obama was considering his run for the Presidency, Michelle famously told him she would give him her blessing only if he agreed to quit smoking, a lifelong on-and-off habit that he had managed to kick for a time but resumed during the stress of the Senate campaign. Down to a few smokes a day by then, he agreed to quit entirely.

Even from afar, Michelle makes sure her husband keeps things in perspective. When he telephoned her from the Capitol to share news of a breakthrough he scored on the Senate Foreign Relations Committee for a bill he was cosponsoring to restrict black-

"It's paparazzi. Stop looking at it."

BARACK OBAMA TO REPORTERS TEASING HIM ABOUT SWIMSUIT PHOTOS

Surfin' U.S.A.: On a beachin' day in Hawaii, Barack Obama got tubular as a tyke (far left); years later, he boogie-boarded with his own kids on a Hawaii vacation during the Christmas holidays of 2006. Just a few weeks later, he revealed that he was going to try to catch a wave that his supporters hope will leave him sittin' on top of the world.

"The euphoria is explosive. We have been so hopeless for the last six years."

MIKE HUXTABLE OF PORTSMOUTH, NEW HAMPSHIRE, WAITING TO SEE OBAMA

"Barack is the most unique political talent I've run into in more than fifty years," said one lifelong Democrat who, like many Obama supporters (at a New Hampshire book-signing in December 2006, top, where buttons were available for sale, above), says he will be a formidable campaigner. "He has the ability to touch diverse crowds," said one, "and there's a sense of clicking."

market arms trade, she interrupted him, he recounts in *The Audacity of Hope*, as he was enthusing about his legislative triumph.

"'We have ants.'

"'Huh?'

"'I found ants in the kitchen. And in the bathroom upstairs...I need you to buy some ant traps on your way home tomorrow.'"

"I hung up the receiver," Obama writes, "wondering if Ted Kennedy or John McCain bought ant traps on the way home from work."

Up until the primary season was in full swing, Obama spent his working weeks in his one bedroom rented apartment on Massachusetts Avenue. He seldom attended the Capitol's glitzier social events when he's in Washington, preferring to join colleagues for bull sessions over beers or steak dinners, discussing, no doubt, politics.

To relax, he worked out at the Senate gym, played basketball or watched games on TV. Often, in the evenings, he jogged to the Washington Monument and sometimes continued on to the Lincoln Memorial and up the stairs to stand at the spot where Martin Luther King Jr. gave his "I Have a Dream" speech in 1963, the Capitol dome shining in the distance.

"And in that place, I think about America and those who built it," he wrote in the closing passages of *The Audacity of Hope*. "And those like Lincoln and King, who ultimately laid down their lives in the service of perfecting an imperfect union...It is that process I wish to be part of.

"My heart is filled with love for this country."

"He realizes that this is his time."

FORMER SENATOR BOB KERREY ON OBAMA

THE ROAD TO THE PRESIDENCY

6

"And that is why, in the shadow of the Old State Capitol, where Lincoln once called on a divided house to stand together, where common hopes and common dreams still live, I stand before you today to announce my candidacy for President of the United States."

With those words, spoken before a cheering crowd on a cold but clear Saturday afternoon in February, 2007, Barack Obama launched what he cast as his own crusade to unite a divided nation. The setting, in the Illinois capitol of Springfield, was significant because, as Obama pointed out, it was there in 1858 that Abraham Lincoln delivered his famous warning that "a house divided against itself cannot stand." The issue then shaking the nation to its very foundations was the institution of slavery. Now, Obama

A crowd of 15,000 braved freezing temperatures to witness the historic launch of Barack Obama's White House bid in Springfield, Ill. As he would do time and again during the upcoming campaign, Obama invoked the legacy of Abe Lincoln, whose own candidacy for the presidency began in Springfield. (Obama speaks in front of the Old State Capitol building, left; a young supporter in Springfield, right; inset: sheet music from Lincoln's 1860 campaign).

said, a new set of issues threatened to divide us. "All of us know what those challenges are today—a war with no end, a dependence on oil that threatens our future, schools where too many children aren't learning, and families struggling paycheck to paycheck despite working as hard as they can."

After enumerating the nation's problems, Obama called upon Americans to unite and work together to find solutions and to achieve Lincoln's "more perfect union."

"I chose to run for the presidency at this moment in history because I believe deeply that we cannot solve the challenges of our time unless we solve them together."

BARACK OBAMA

Throughout his speech, Obama invoked Illinois' favorite son as the crowd responded with wave after enthusiastic wave of rousing cheers:

"As Lincoln organized the forces arrayed against slavery, he was heard to say: 'Of strange, discordant, and even hostile elements, we gathered from the four winds, and formed and fought to battle through.' That is our purpose here today. That's why I'm in this race. Not just to hold an office, but to gather with you to transform a nation…

"And if you will join me in this improbable quest…then I'm ready to take up the cause, and march with you, and work with you. Together, starting today, let us finish the work that needs to be done, and usher in a new birth of freedom on this Earth."

In the Land of Lincoln, Obama's repeated references to the man he at one point called "a tall, gangly, self-made Springfield lawyer," certainly resonated. And many in his audience may well have realized, as Obama no doubt intended, that despite their obvious differences, the white Republican 16th president and the African-American Democrat who hoped to become the 44th had more in common than their physical stature, professional background, and adopted home state.

Like Obama, Lincoln served four terms in the Illinois legislature before he ran for national office. Elected to the House of Representatives in 1846, he served a single term in Washington. Like Obama, Lincoln was an outspoken critic of a war being waged by an unpopular president.

Obama's opposition to the war in Iraq lifted him to political prominence in Illinois, where it was highly unpopular. But Lincoln's harsh condemnation of President James Polk's Mexican War did not sit well with constituents back home, and he did not run for reelection in 1848.

Ten years later, Lincoln ran for the U.S. Senate. (The famous "house divided" address in Springfield to which Obama alluded launched Lincoln's 1858 Senate campaign). But unlike Obama, who won his Senate race in 2004, Lincoln lost.

Two years later, when Lincoln ran for president, his primary opponent for his party's nomination was a U.S. Senator from New York State. William H. Seward, eight years Lincoln's elder and a former governor of New York, as well as its sitting Senator, had a long and distinguished career as a public servant and was a well-known national figure.

In Lincoln, a loser on the national stage

just two years before, Seward seemed to have an unworthy opponent, a greenhorn from the provinces known for his gifted oratory and little else. Seward could easily paint Lincoln as unfit to be his party's standard bearer, with little or no chance to win. If Lincoln wasn't too young to be president (he was 51 when he ran; Obama will be 47 on Inauguration Day, 2009), he was certainly far too inexperienced to serve as commander-in-chief at such a critical time in the nation's history.

Lincoln, of course, won the nomination and went on to win the general election.

Now, 147 years (or seven score and seven years, to use a certain famous rhetorical device) after Lincoln embarked from Springfield on his own "improbable quest," Obama, the "tall, gangly" single-term junior Senator from Illinois faced similar questions about his maturity, his experience and his fitness to be president in a time of war—all soon to be posed by the New York Senator who would be his principle opponent in his fight for his party's nomination.

Little wonder then that Obama invoked the Great Emancipator in his historic announcement as the crowd of supporters in Springfield chanted "Obama! Obama!"

"He had his doubts. He had his defeats. He had his setbacks, but through his will and his words, he moved a nation and helped free a people," Obama said of Lincoln.

As would happen time and again during the ensuing campaign, many in the crowd

"I see him as a leader, rather than a boss," Craigslist founder Craig Newmark, said of Obama (in Springfield, Feb. 10, 2007). A leader, he said, inspires supporters to help him get things done, while a boss "can order you to do things, sure, but you do them because it's part of the contract."

were as stirred by the emotion-packed symbolism of the moment as by the words of the candidate who could become the first black president. Months later, after hearing Obama speak for the first time, a woman in Texas expressed what many among the multitudes who turned out to hear him all along the campaign trail felt.

"For me, in my lifetime," the woman told a *Washington Post* reporter, "it is truly possible that an African-American man can be the president of the United States. My family, my mother, my aunts, my uncles, might get to see that in their lifetime. That makes me almost want to cry just thinking about it."

After his campaign kickoff speech, Obama left Springfield and crossed the Mississippi to Iowa, where the first votes in the Democratic Party caucuses would be cast nearly a year later, on January 3, 2008.

In his wake, Obama left some listeners eager to pledge their support. "We need

(At left) Obama talks to reporters aboard a plane en route to a campaign stop Tuesday, Jan. 1, 2008, in Sioux City, Iowa. His wife said, "If Barack doesn't win Iowa, it is just a dream." Obama at a campaign stop in Cedar Rapids, Iowa, on January 2, 2008, the last day before the Iowa caucus (above).

this guy," a man with a heavy "da Bears" Chicago accent said as the crowd dispersed. "Our nation needs this guy."

Said another, "I'll walk to Iowa, if I have to, to help this man."

Obama himself did not have to make the trek on foot of course. But for all the euphoria of his supporters, he faced daunting odds as he headed to Iowa, a state where blacks make up a meager 2.5 percent of the population. Polls conducted just four months before showed that a sizable portion of the nation's voting public—a whopping 37 percent—had no idea who Barack Obama even was. Among likely Democratic voters, fewer than 10 percent considered him a viable candidate.

As her campaign progressed, Hillary Clinton (introduced by her hubby at an Iowa rally in July, 2007, left) made improvements to her Web site (below). But in the early stages of the campaign, she was hard pressed to keep up with Obama, who raised record amounts of money on line. His Web site (right) is "far more dynamic than any of the others," Bentley College media professor Christine Williams told *Fast Company* magazine.

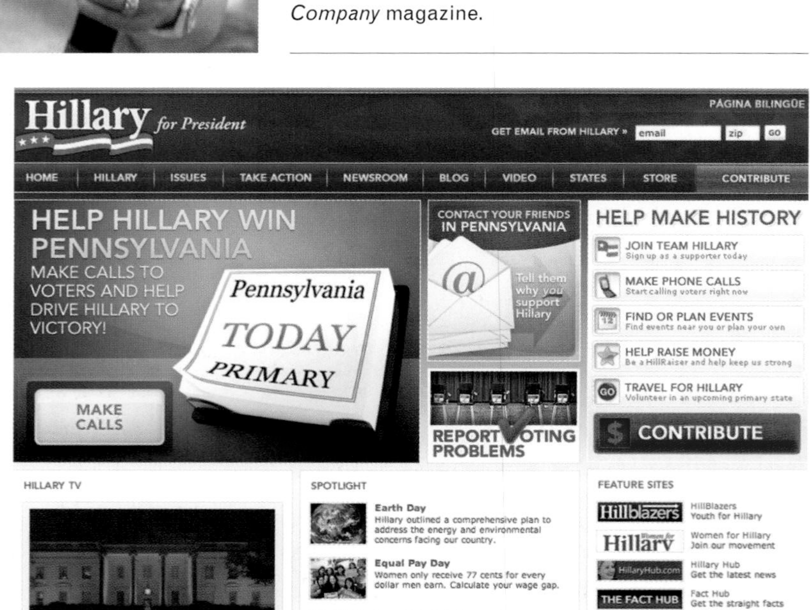

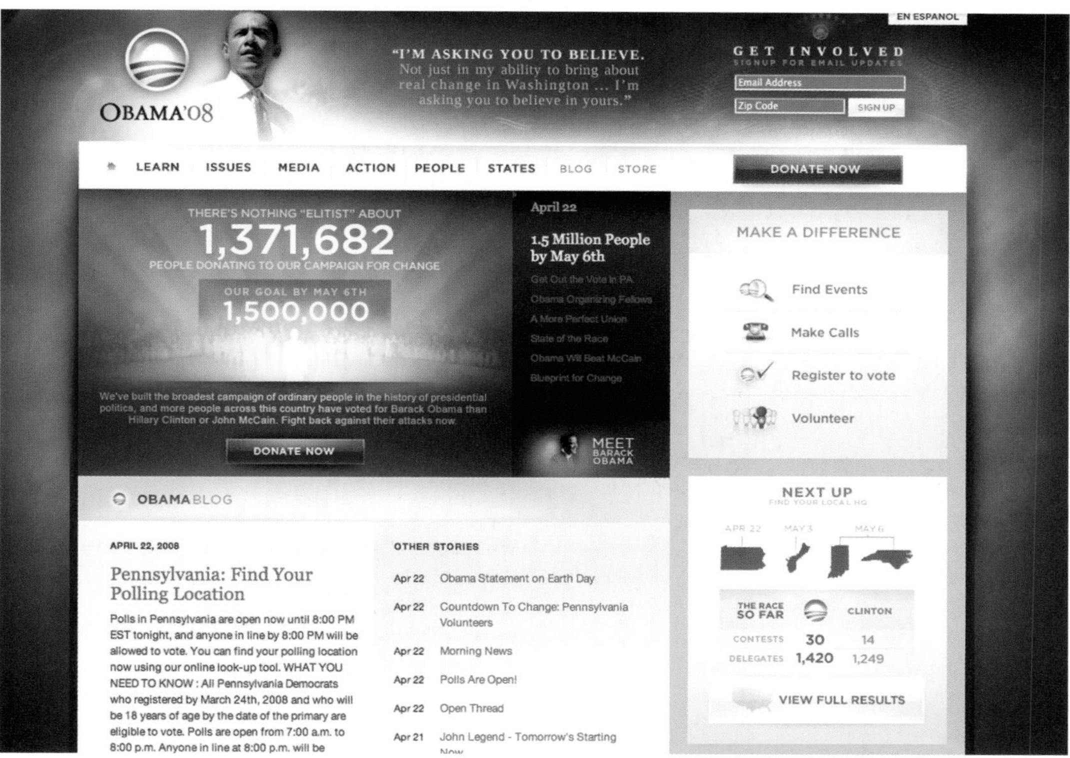

New York Senator Hillary Clinton, herself on an historic quest to become the first female president, led a field of candidates, most much better-known than Obama, by a wide margin.

Back in the fall of 2006, as Obama crisscrossed the nation campaigning for Democrats in the mid-term elections and then again on his book tour, buzz had begun to build in anticipation of his becoming a candidate for president. When he told reporters that he was indeed contemplating a run, polls showed a surge of support among likely voters.

But the giddy expectations of supporters were wildly out of sync with reality, according to Political Arithmetic, a website that tracks polling trends. While surveys showed that Obama's support had risen to an impressive 17 percent, the site's analyst stated, "Any sensible reading of these data show that while Sen. Obama has enjoyed a brief flurry of attention, he is far from catching up to the actual front runner, Sen. Clinton, whose most recent polls are over twice as high."

Obama faced more than just a formidable campaigner in Hillary Clinton. Also marshaled against him was the well-oiled organizational and fund-raising apparatus first built by her husband. The Clinton machine had been tested and proven victorious in Bill Clinton's two presidential campaigns and Hillary's two Senate campaigns.

As Obama said in a *New York Times* interview, his opponent's very name, beloved by Democrats, was a challenge in itself: "We're running against the most established brand in the Democratic Party for the last two decades."

Even so, Obama's campaign had a new and different kind of political organization already in place the day he announced that

WE CAN BELI
WWW.BARACKOBAMA.COM
CHANGE
WE CAN
BELIEVE IN
CHANGE
WE CAN
BELIEVE IN

he was running. A savvy, sophisticated, and highly effective Internet presence included a visitor-friendly campaign Web site (barackobama.com), as well as a cluster of related social networking sites developed in part by Facebook cofounder Chris Hughes. Obama immediately began organizing supporters, fielding volunteers and raising bushels of money not only among the corn fields of Iowa, but in primary states all across the country.

Time magazine called the role of the Internet in the 2008 election "the biggest shift in national politics since the rise of television. For millions of Americans, the Internet has turned presidential politics into a fully interactive event, a chance to give money with mouse clicks and to volunteer virtually from miles away."

No campaign was more adept at using the new technology than Obama's, *Time* declared. Through its easily navigated Web site, supporters were able to download phone lists of likely voters, organize groups of volunteers to canvas neighborhoods or just meet to chat about what they liked about Obama.

In key primary states, *Time* reported, by the time "the first paid operatives arrived in the area...a virtually organized Obama machine [was] already up and running."

For example, the *Washington Post* reported, Texas' largest online grass roots organizing networks, Austin for Obama and San Antonio for Obama (as well as similar virtual groups in other big cities), "were created on Feb. 10, 2007, the day Obama announced his White House bid."

"Yes We Can!" the on-line "mashup" created by the Black Eyed Peas' leader will.i.am (left, with Live's Ed Kowalczyk at an Obama rally), starred a host of well-known musicians and celebrities who intoned Obama's campaign slogan. Produced independently, it "cost the campaign nothing and became a viral hit," noted *Fast Company* magazine's Ellen McGirt.

Voters were able to study Obama's stance on issues and check out his speeches on his website. They can also follow a link to watch the so-called viral video "Yes We Can," by hip hop artist and Obama supporter will.i.am on YouTube. Obama fans could find networks of like-minded folks on Facebook, LinkedIn, and MySpace. One Obama volunteer told the *Post* that the Internet was not only her favorite means of following the campaign; it was her only source for political news. She had no use for media that wasn't interactive, she said, adding that she only turned on her television to watch DVDs.

For the Clinton campaign, Obama's virtual head start meant playing catch up. Quoting Simon Rosenberg, a veteran of Bill Clinton's campaigns who now runs the New Democrat Network, the *Post* said that Sen. Clinton's campaign "found itself stuck in the 20th-century model of campaigning: the 30-second TV spot, a tarmac stop and 200 kids in the headquarters."

Obama's campaign was more 21st century, the *Post* reported: "Everyday, because of the Internet, supporters work for their candidates, contacting their friends on various sites, sending e-mails, watching and creating videos, and forwarding them online."

Said Rosenberg: "The Clinton campaign missed the zeitgeist of the moment." And, he added, they "underestimated the possible reach of Obama's support, and they're paying for it."

The fundraising power of Obama's Internet effort was first glimpsed during the opening months of his campaign.

In Iowa, his ability to draw enthusiastic, widely diverse crowds was quickly confirmed as supporters and the merely curious flocked to hear him speak or simply to get a look at the charismatic candidate. Everyone in politics quickly recognized that Obama was an extraordinary campaigner as well as an inspiring speechmaker. At the end of June, they found out that he was also a money magnet beyond compare.

In the first quarter of 2007, his campaign reported that he had raised $24.8 million, an amount not to be sneezed at. But then, three months later, came the announcement that the total haul for the first six months of the year was a staggering $58 million, more cash than any candidate had ever raised during a six-month period in a non-election year.

It was a fundraising achievement that Obama's campaign manager, David Plouffe crowed, was "something no presidential campaign has ever dreamed of at this stage." More than 250,000 individual donors contributed, many of them young, internet-savvy political novices who had never donated to a campaign before, Plouffe added. The result demonstrated, he said, "that our movement is both bigger and deeper than anything presidential politics has ever seen."

And Obama was only just getting started. Impressive as the number of donors and amount of money raised was, the figures would be dwarfed by what was to come.

"If Hillary Clinton is the nominee," Obama (debating Clinton in New Hampshire) told the *New York Times*, "there's not going to be an expansion of the electorate. I am convinced that I've got the capacity to attract independents and Republicans in a way that she can't do."

"You've got at least eight Democrats running for the presidency," Obama mused in the late fall of 2006 after he had let it be known that he was likely to join the race with fellow Senators Clinton, John Edwards, Joe Biden, and Christopher Dodd, as well as former Senator Mike Gravel of Alaska, Ohio Representative Dennis Kucinich and Governor Bill Richardson of New Mexico. "I'd say we're gonna have some silly season goin' on."

But the mood around Obama's Iowa campaign headquarters in the summer of 2007 was anything but lighthearted in the aftermath of the first series of Democratic debates. Commentators judged that Obama had stumbled badly in April during the first debate, held in Orangeburg, South Carolina. His response to a question about how he would react to a surprise terror attack was so lame, opined *Time* magazine's Karen Tumulty, he sounded "more like a candidate to head the volunteer fire department as [his answer] focused on disaster preparedness."

Clinton, by contrast, Tumulty noted, "spoke as a Commander in Chief: 'I think a President must move as swiftly as is prudent to retaliate.'"

Despite pleas from his frustrated staff to respond to Clinton's jabs that he was too inexperienced and immature to accept the responsibilities of the Oval Office, Obama refused to strike back. "That's not who I am," he told advisors who begged him to "punch harder."

Unable "to put much of a dent in Hillary Clinton's trajectory of preordination and inevitability," Tumulty wrote, Obama "appeared destined for the same fate that had met a long line of Democratic insurgents—Gary Hart, Paul Tsongas, Bill Bradley, and Howard Dean among them." Those candidates' "promises of a new kind of politics had briefly enjoyed a vogue," she pointed out, "only to be crushed into dust by a front-runner who was using the standard playbook."

In an interview with the *New York Times*, Obama admitted he was disappointed in his early performance. "I think there's no doubt that in the first couple of debates, the format didn't work for me. Or I didn't adapt to the format."

"So when I talk about real change that will make a real difference in the lives of working families—change that will restore balance in our economy and put us on a path to prosperity—it's not just the poll-tested rhetoric of a political campaign. It's the cause of my life. And you can be sure that it will be the cause of my presidency from the very first day I take office."

BARACK OBAMA

Yet, he said, "I am not interested in tearing into Hillary Clinton. I think she is an admirable person [and] a capable senator....That doesn't mean that we don't both defend ourselves against attack."

Obama's civility seemed to translate to audiences as a kind of above-it-all detachment. A top campaign advisor told *Time*

that during the summer of 2007 there was a feeling of "panic" among Obama's aides. "They said 'he's gotta engage.'"

In the autumn, he finally did. In speeches and interviews, Obama began to argue that it was Clinton, not he, who would be unelectable in November, 2008. He told the *New York Times* that Clinton could not deliver the kind of change in Washington that voters desperately want. "I don't think people know what her agenda is," he said. "[T]here has been a tendency to

go back and forth in her positions."

On the offensive now, Obama accused Clinton of using the same kind of "triangulating and poll-driven positions" that marked her husband's politics in the 1990s. Particularly on the war in Iraq, she had continually

"Barack Obama is three things you want in a brand," marketing executive Keith Reinhard told *Fast Company* magazine. "New, different, and attractive. That's as good as it gets." (Here, Obama stands out from the crowd the first Democratic primary debate in South Carolina on April 26, 2007).

"I believe the biggest issue today is the danger we face overseas," said one New York City woman who switched her support from Clinton to Obama (speaking in South Carolina) on primary day. "It's going to be a lot harder for Osama Bin Laden to convince kids in Pakistan to hate a country that elects a black man with an African name president. `Death to America? I don't think so.'"

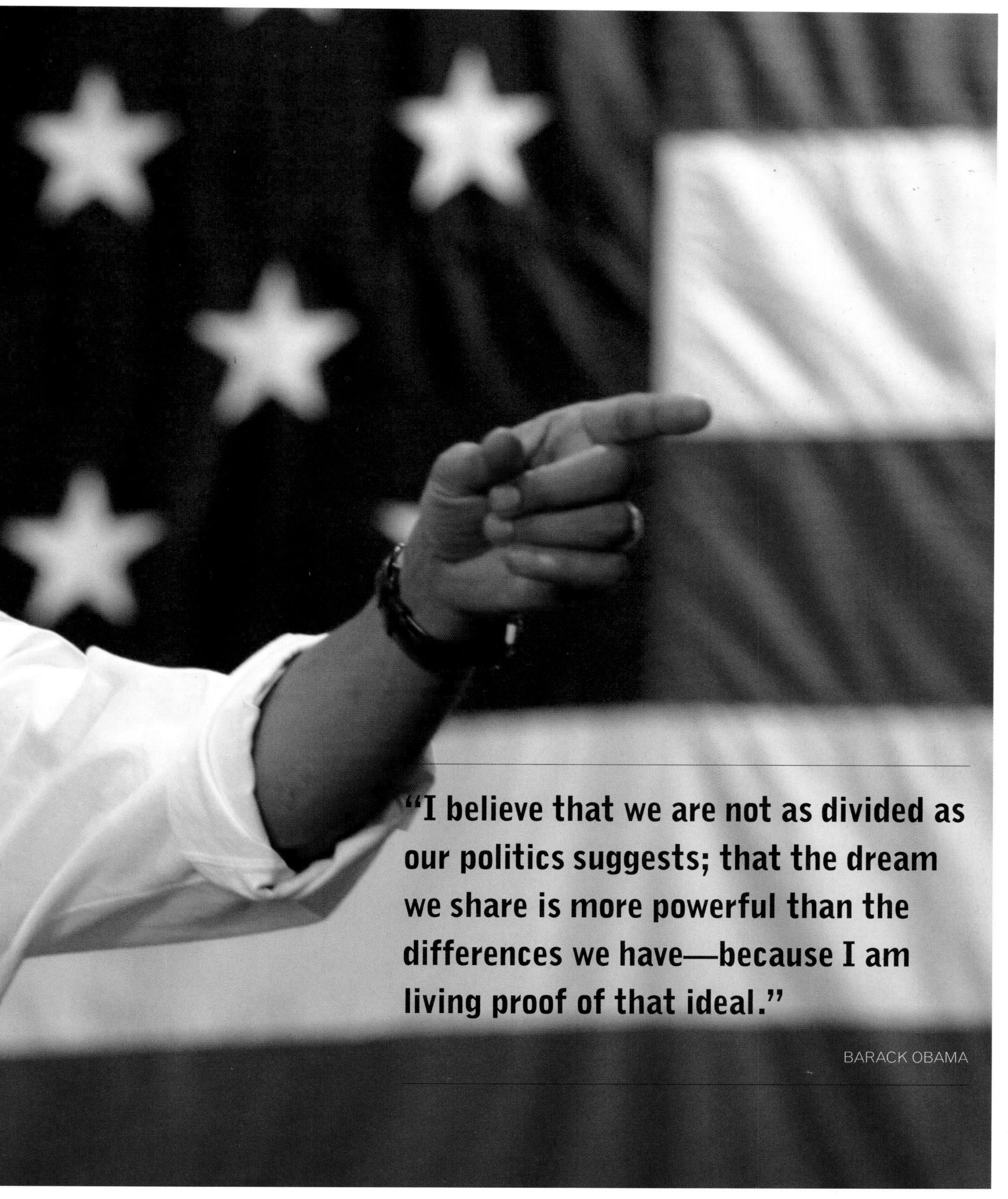

"I believe that we are not as divided as our politics suggests; that the dream we share is more powerful than the differences we have—because I am living proof of that ideal."

BARACK OBAMA

Obama's surprising victory in Iowa was "a defining moment in history," the former underdog exulted in Des Moines on caucus night (left, with his wife, Michelle, and daughters Malia, left, and Sasha). The next day, Clinton spoke in New Hampshire (right), where her victory in the following week's primary temporarily shifted momentum in her favor.

hedged her bets, Obama charged. "I continue to believe that on the biggest foreign policy disaster of a generation, she got it wrong and I got it right," he told the *Times*.

Obama's new aggressiveness thrilled his staff. "There's a certain joy I see in him now," campaign strategist David Axelrod told *Time*. "I just sensed that sort of incredible focus, energy, acuity, joy [that had been missing early on]. He's into it."

While voters responded in kind, pushing Obama's poll numbers higher and cutting into Clinton's at the same time, Democratic Party leaders cautioned him. "He has to be very careful about how he attacks her," former Al Gore campaign manager Donna Brazile told *Time*. "I am not convinced [Obama's] campaign has any sense of how hard the Clintons fight when they feel their birthright is being challenged. I am not sure they are ready for this."

After a debate in which her opponents seemed to gang up on her, Clinton complained to CBS's Katie Couric that the press had given the other candidates, particularly Obama, "free rein" to go after her. "After you've been attacked as often as I have from several of my opponents, you can't just absorb it—you have to respond."

The sparring that would, depending on one's point of view, either mar or enliven the campaign throughout the months ahead, had begun in earnest. When Clinton said that if elected she, unlike Obama, would not need on-the-job training in economic policy, Obama shot back: "I am happy to compare my experiences with hers when it comes to the economy. My understanding was that she wasn't Treasury Secretary in the Clinton administration."

Clinton's campaign was scornful of Obama's new attack strategy. "They've junked the politics of hope," Clinton spokesman Howard Wolfson told *Time*. "His whole brand is based on that."

Obama responded in the *Times*: "I've been amused by seeing some of the commentary out of the Clinton camp, where every time we point out a difference between me and her, they say 'What happened to the politics of hope?' which is just silly. The notion that somehow changing tone means simply that we let them say whatever they want to say; or that we're all holding hands and singing 'Kumbaya' is obviously not how I function. Hope is not ignoring differences or ignoring problems."

Polls showed Obama catching and even pulling ahead of Clinton in Iowa and gaining strongly on her in New Hampshire, where the first ballots would be cast in the primaries on January 8, just five days after Iowa's town-meeting style caucuses. Obama campaigned in both states in the last week of 2007. His armies of volunteers were making 10,000 phone calls a night to Democrats, urging them to speak up for their candidate on caucus night. Obama still considered the race so tight, according to one news report, he telephoned local caucus leaders, including county sheriffs and other town officials as he campaigned across the state.

As 2007 drew to a close, Obama had been campaigning in Iowa and elsewhere for nearly a year. He and his Democratic rivals had participated in ten nationally televised debates, with seven more scheduled for the first two months of 2008. "We've played four quarters and now the game is just beginning," Obama advisor David Axelrod said in a *New York Times* interview.

The once relatively leisurely pace of the primary season, which unfolded slowly after

With electrifying charisma, Obama (campaigning in New Jersey on the eve of February's Super Tuesday primaries, below) is able to reach voters as no politican has since Jack and Bobby Kennedy, supporters say. When their younger brother Teddy endorsed Obama (in Washington, January 28, 2008, right), Obama praised Kennedy, hailing him as "the lion of the Senate" and "a champion for working Americans, a fierce proponent of universal health care, and a tireless advocate for giving every child in this country a quality education." Republicans will no doubt use the candidate's embrace of Kennedy as ammunition in their own campaign to paint Obama as too liberal for mainstream Americans.

Iowa and New Hampshire, had been replaced by a front-loaded process that would send voters from more than 30 states to the polls in the first five weeks of the new year.

"Now," Axelrod said, "you have a situation where you campaign for a full year, and then the process is compressed into a few frenetic weeks."

When *Time* prodded Obama to critique the "long and brutal" primary process, he said he had no problems with it.

"Ultimately, the process reveals aspects of an individual's character and judgment," he said. "Those two things, along with vision, are the most important aspect of a presidency. 'Do you know where you want

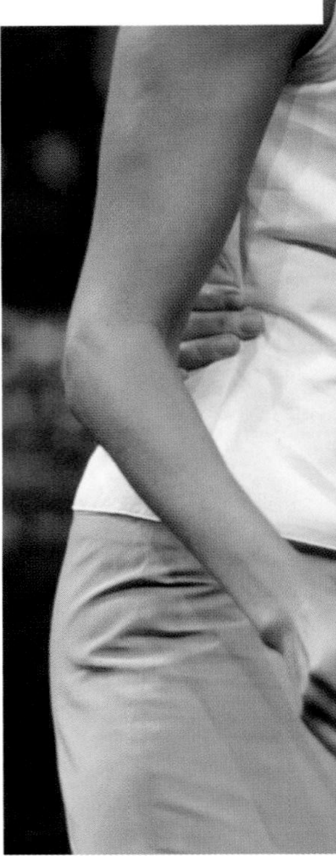

to take the country? Do you have the judgment to figure out what's important and what's not? Do you have the character to withstand trials and tribulations and to bounce back from setbacks?'"

In the first several months of the grueling election year ahead, Obama's response to those very questions would be put to the severest tests.

After 11 exhausting months of nonstop campaigning, the election year had finally dawned. And for Barack Obama and his supporters, it got off to a stirring start with his electrifying win in the Iowa caucuses on

A crowd of 20,000 greeted Obama in Minnesota, left, and Michelle Obama was joined by Caroline Kennedy, California first lady Maria Shriver and Oprah Winfrey at a rally in Los Angeles February 3, 2008.

January 3. His convincing victory in the overwhelmingly white state of Iowa, wrote *Washington Post* columnist Eugene Robinson, "showed us the America we like to believe we live in.

"It was one of those moments that give you goose bumps—the cheering crowd, the waving placards, the candidate and his family looking Kennedyesque on the occasion of a stunning victory."

"They said this day would never come," Obama declared in his victory speech. Indeed, just seven years before he had been told to shelve his political aspirations in the aftermath of the terror attacks of September 11, 2001. American voters, it seemed then, would not elect anyone named Barack Hussein Obama to a village council much less the presidency of the United States.

When the voters of Iowa put him on the path that could lead to that seemingly unreachable goal, it was, Obama proclaimed, a "defining moment in [American] history."

But the euphoria of his victory splintered in the cold of New Hampshire just five days later with Hillary Clinton's equally surprising victory in a state pollsters had predicted Obama would win on the strength of his Iowa momentum. Instead, exit polling suggested, Clinton had ridden "a wave of female support" triggered by a frank and emotionally honest conversation she'd had with voters on the eve of balloting.

Thereafter, the momentum continued to swing back and forth between the two rival candidates like a metronome, with the former first lady's surging support carrying her to victories in Michigan and Nevada before Obama bounced back with what the press termed "a commanding victory" in South Carolina.

"We leave this great state with the wind at our backs," Obama exulted.

And it seemed so when, days later, in an emotion-packed news conference, Sen. Ted Kennedy passed the mantle of his martyred brothers to the candidate who had so often been compared to them. "There was another time, when another young candidate was running for president and challenging America to cross a new frontier," Kennedy said, invoking the themes of his late brother's campaign as JFK's daughter Caroline stood at his side. "He faced criticism from the preceding Democratic president, who was widely respected in the party. And John Kennedy replied: 'The world is changing. The old ways will not do. It is time for a new generation of leadership.'

"So it is with Barack Obama."

But again, Obama's momentum seemed to stall.

The expected final showdown on Super Tuesday, the mother of all primary days on February 5, when voters in more than 20 states and protectorates cast their ballots, failed to produce a clear winner. When the smoke cleared, Clinton had won the biggest prize, California, as well as Massachusetts, despite the Kennedy family's endorsement of Obama. Both candidates had bragging rights, however. Obama won more states, 13 to Clinton's 8. While Clinton gained a slight edge in the overall battle for delegates, with 892 total compared to Obama's 716, neither candidate was close to the 2,025 needed to win the nomination.

Over the course of the next few weeks however, the momentum seemed to swing again in Obama's favor. He continued to draw large and enthusiastic crowds whenever he spoke. Supporters wearing "Barack

Going into the crucial Pennsylvania primary, polls showed that Obama (with U.S. Steel workers in Pennsylvania) was not only running behind Clinton, but behind John McCain among white male voters, who favored the Republican by a daunting 57 to 33 percent nationwide, according to *New York* magazine.

'n Roll" pins encouraged reporters to once again compare Obama's reception at rallies to "a rock star's welcome." (Fittingly, on February 10, Obama was awarded his second Grammy, for his spoken word recording of *The Audacity of Hope*). By the end of the month, he had swept 11 straight primaries and caucuses and had overtaken Clinton in the all-important race for delegates.

As the contest moved to the crucial states of Texas and Ohio, where primaries on March 4 would, experts predicted, finally bring the drama to a conclusion once and for all, Obama's supporters were speaking of the candidate with almost religious fervor.

"Whether or not he wins the nomination, whether or not he makes it all the way to the White House," an Obama volunteer in Texas told the *Washington Post*, "this is a movement. A movement is when you're emotionally involved and that's where I am."

Said Georgia Congressman John Lewis, who switched his support from Clinton to Obama on the eve of the March 4 primaries: "His rise is the most moving and exciting political movement that I've seen in my lifetime." Those were words of high praise indeed coming as they did from Lewis, a leader of The Movement, the civil rights crusade of the 1960s.

But when the votes were tallied, Clinton had won the two battleground states of Texas and Ohio. "No candidate in recent history—Democratic or Republican—has won the White House without winning the Ohio primary," Clinton reminded supporters at her victory rally.

But despite the losses, Obama still held the lead in delegates, thanks to victories in Vermont and the caucus portion of the Texas primary.

Days after the primary, the Federal Election Commission released figures that

RICA
AD 1590

The controversy sparked by incendiary remarks made by Rev. Jeremiah Wright (with Obama in 2005) on the eve of the Pennsylvania primary were quickly exploited by conservative attack specialists. One such group posted an anti-Obama video on YouTube that featured film of the candidate backed by a soundtrack created by splicing Wright's rants and edgy hip hop beats by the rap group Public Enemy. "Expect more from the shadowy world of 527s that disgorged the Swift Boat Veterans for Truth," wrote *New York* magazine's John Heilemann, referring to the well-funded campaign to discredit Kerry's exemplary war record during the 2004 campaign.

showed that another kind of momentum—money—was definitely in Obama's favor.

His campaign, the FEC reported, had raised an astounding $55 million in February, a record for a single month by any presidential candidate ever. Once again, the figure proved the fund raising potency of Obama's campaign, which filled its coffers with contributions from 727,972 individual donors in February alone. To date, Obama had received donations from almost 1.5 million supporters, far more than any other candidate, according to the *Los Angeles Times.*

With subsequent wins in Wyoming and Mississippi, Obama began to pick up endorsements from many of the so-called super delegates, party luminaries and Democratic elected officials whose votes could prove the difference in determining who would win the nomination at the Democratic convention in August.

Once again momentum seemed to be shifting toward Obama as he and Clinton turned their attention to Pennsylvania, the last big primary battle—and possibly the decisive one—before the Convention.

Then, the political equivalent of a tsunami struck. The trigger, like an undersea earthquake thousands of miles distant, was a series of years-old sermons by Obama's pastor, the Rev. Jeremiah Wright, which had been taped at his Trinity United Church of Christ in Chicago shortly after the 2001 terror attacks. "God damn America," Wright bellowed on the tapes that were replayed over and over on television.

The shock waves threatened to derail a campaign that until then had been praised for its smooth-running efficiency.

Obama responded by delivering a moving and powerful speech on March 18, in which he used the Wright controversy to address the divisive issue of race.

While condemning Wright's words, Obama attributed them to feelings of bitterness and anger that were deep rooted and widespread among blacks as a result of the terrible legacies of slavery and segregation. For Wright and his generation, "the memories of humiliation and doubt and fear have not gone away," Obama said.

White Americans should keep that in mind, he suggested, just as blacks should realize that whites feel embittered as well "when they are told to bus their children to a school across town; when they hear that an African American is getting an advantage in landing a good job...when they're told that their fears about crime in urban neighborhoods are somehow prejudiced."

The widely and extravagantly praised speech seemed to defuse the crisis at first. But for Obama and his supporters, there was a painful irony to contemplate: The campaign that Obama had kicked off the year before by invoking Lincoln's "a house divided cannot stand" speech was threatened a year later by the divisive and explosive issue of racism, the roots of which were

ultimately entangled with the very issue—slavery—that Lincoln had addressed in Springfield exactly 150 years before.

"Contrary to the claims of some of my critics, black and white, I have never been so naïve as to believe that we can get beyond our racial divisions in a single election cycle, or with a single candidacy—particularly a candidacy as imperfect as my own."

BARACK OBAMA

No sooner had Obama seemed to recover than another, related controversy erupted. In addressing supporters at a San Francisco fund raiser, he again spoke of the bitterness of working class whites whose resentments and frustrations caused them

---

Flanked by Old Glory as he delivered his moving and insightful speech on race in Philadelphia March 18, Obama seemed to weather the storm unleashed by Rev. Wright. But in April, in the aftermath of his loss in the Pennsylvania primary and faced with yet another crucial series of supposed make-or-break primaries in Indiana and North Carolina, Wright repeated many of his most controversial statements in a much publicized press tour. In response, Obama, whose association with the pastor who married him and baptized his children made opponents question his patriotism as well as his judgment, angrily disowned Wright in an April 29 speech in which he said that the preacher's comments were "divisive and destructive" and "an insult to what we've been trying to do in this campaign."

After John McCain clinched his party's nomination in Florida (above), the increasingly divisive fight between Clinton and Obama (at at Texas rally, right) caused Republicans to exult. "The Democrats are destroying themselves," a GOP strategist told *New York*'s Heilemann. "They're engaged in killing Obama. It's like killing Santa Claus on Christmas morning – the kids won't forget or forgive." Said Republican guru Karl Rove: "About twice as many Democrats support McCain as Republicans support Obama, and about three times as many Democrats support McCain as Republicans support Clinton. The media is all wired about thsese `Obamacans,'" Rove said in a speech in March. "The real story of this election is the `McCainocrats.'

"to cling to guns or religion or antipathy to people who aren't like them…as a way to express their frustrations."

Hillary Clinton was not alone in condemning the remark, which fellow Democrats and commentators on both sides of the political divide loudly denounced as evidence that Obama was elitist and woefully out of touch with working people.

"No, I'm in touch," Obama said at a campaign rally after the presumed Republican nominee John McCain had joined the chorus of condemnation. "I know exactly what's going on. People are fed up, they're angry, they're frustrated, they're bitter and they want to see a change in Washington."

When voters went to the polls in Pennsylvania on April 22, less than two weeks after the "bitter" controversy erupted, they gave Clinton a decisive win. Despite the victory, her quest to become the first female nominee remained stalled. Though she beat Obama by nearly 10 percentage points in the voting, the 85 delegates she won outnumbered Obama's apportioned share by a mere dozen. Cheered as she was by the results, Clinton faced campaign budget short falls, as well as an uphill battle to overtake her opponent, who led in the all-important race for the 2,118 delegates needed for the nomination.

Two weeks later, on May 6, Clinton added the Indiana primary to her string of electoral victories. But the win—by a mere two percentage points in a state she was expected to carry by a far-wider margin—was less than resounding. On the same day, Obama scored a decisive double-digit victory in North Carolina, leading respected NBC political analyst Tim Russert to declare the contest essentially over. Clinton, Russert said on-air, "did not get the game-changer she wanted tonight. We now know who the Democratic nominee will be."

Barack Obama's stunning achievement would not become official until June 3,

CHANGE
CHANGE
CHANGE

when his win in the Montana primary—and a simultaneous rush by a flock of superdelegates to his banner—guaranteed that he would be the first black major party presidential candidate in American history.

"You chose not to listen to your doubts or your fears, but to your greatest hopes and aspirations," Obama said with Lincolnesque eloquence at a rally in Minnesota that night. "Because of you," he told supporters, "I can stand before you and say that I will be the Democratic nominee for president of the United States."

Whether or not Obama would succeed in his historic quest, it was certain that his campaign, in which the son of a white mother and a black father appealed, like Lincoln, to the American people to band together and build a more perfect union, had already contributed a stirring and dramatic chapter to the history of American presidential politics.

"This fall," Obama said in a rousing primary victory speech May 6 in North Carolina (left) that signaled his emergence as the presumed nominee, "we intend to march forward as one Democratic Party, united by a common vision for this country. Because we all agree that at this defining moment in history—a moment when we're facing two wars, an economy in turmoil, a planet in peril—we can't afford to give John McCain the chance to serve out George Bush's third term. We need change in America."

THE HISTORIC ELECTION

(Left) Following his acceptance speech, Obama introduced Michelle as "our next first lady." The four-day Democratic National Convention was the most widely seen since the Nielsen ratings began measuring convention audiences in 1960, when Democrats nominated John F. Kennedy. (Top) "Our party and our country are better off because of her," Obama said of Hillary Clinton during his acceptance speech in Denver. "And I am a better candidate for having had the honor to compete [with her]." Rousing speeches by Hillary and Bill Clinton helped draw record audiences for the convention telecast and at other rallies, like this one in Florida on October 20. (Bottom) By the last weeks of October, support for Obama seemed to be snowballing, with the Democrat making in-roads in states like Missouri, where a supporter displayed her enthusiasm at an Obama rally under the Gateway Arch at the Jefferson National Expansion Memorial in St. Louis.

7

On June 3, 2008, the day he locked up the Democratic presidential nomination, Barack Obama stood on stage in the Xcel Energy Center in St. Paul, Minnesota, the very venue where, three months later, the Republican Party would convene to nominate Arizona Senator John Sidney McCain III as its candidate for president. There Obama fired the opening salvos in what was about to become one of the most momentous, contentious, tense, transfixing, and at times flat-out bizarre general elections in modern American history.

Already, the race was one for the ages, pitting the unlikeliest of candidates—an until-recently barely known freshman Senator from Illinois, whose color and very name seemed to disqualify him from serious contention—against a former Congressman and four-term U.S. Senator who was one of the most familiar faces in American politics.

A decorated war hero and P. O. W. who spent six years in a North Vietnamese prison camp, McCain had scored a back-from-the-dead March victory in the Republican primaries that had been hailed as nothing short of a political miracle. Older (by 25 years), presumably wiser and certainly far more experienced a campaigner than Obama, he had a three-month head start to get a seemingly sure-fire, "Count-on-McCain-in-a-Time-of-War" candidacy on target.

If Obama felt exhausted from his knockdown, drag-out with Hillary Clinton, a year-and-a-half marathon that had drawn more voters to the polls and proven longer, more expensive and more draining than ever anyone predicted, he didn't show it.

Obama stood smiling on a stage festooned with enormous American flags and draped in patriotic bunting, with music blaring from huge speakers and the cheers of his supporters, an army 18,000 strong, ringing from the rafters of the jam-packed sports arena

After paying tribute to fallen comrades, lavishing special praise on the fiercest and most tenacious of his vanquished primary foes, Hillary Clinton, Obama rolled out his campaign's big guns. He hammered the issues that he and his fellow Democrats counted on to carry the day in November—the economy, the Bush administration's disastrous mismanagement of it, and McCain's support of Republican policies that favored the wealthy and big business at the expense of middle class working families.

"In just a few short months, the Republican party will arrive in St. Paul with a very different agenda," Obama said. "They will come here to nominate John McCain, a man who has served this country heroically. My differences with him are not personal; they are the policies he has proposed in this campaign."

As adamantly as his opponent tried to sell himself as a Republican "maverick" and a courageous agent of change in Washington, McCain was, Obama reminded his listeners, a staunch supporter of the sitting, highly unpopular Republican president. Rather than opposing the administration's failed economic policies, he had voted with his party 95 percent of the time Congress was

in session during the previous year. "There are many words to describe John McCain's attempt to pass off his embrace of George Bush's policies as bipartisan and new," he said, "but 'change' is not one of them."

Even with the looming credit and stock market crisis still months away, the majority of Americans were already identifying the economy as the number one election-year issue. Ironically, the Iraq War, the issue that had thrust the anti-war Illinois state senator to political prominence, was no longer foremost on voters' minds. Though opinion polls showed that most Americans opposed the war, it was relegated to the campaign's back burners, another tragic example, like the administration's response to Hurricane Katrina, of failed governance.

Days after claiming victory in St. Paul, Obama began a two-week cross-country tour in which he spoke almost exclusively on economic issues, tying McCain in his stump speeches to tax cut-and-run policies of the Bush administration. "For all his talk of independence, the centerpiece of his economic plan amounts to a full-throated endorsement of George Bush's policies," Obama told crowds in Raleigh, North Carolina.

Obama would stay on message and ride it all the way to the White House. His words resonated even in states like Virginia, the heart of old secessionist Dixie, where Obama's distant relative, Jefferson Davis, served as chief executive of the slave-holding Confederate States of America. "I think he can turn this into a 'blue' state," said one young Virginian who arrived at a rally to hear Obama speak and ended up volunteering to work for his campaign.

"His policies are what we need," said an 18-year-old first time voter from Manassas, the site of the pivotal Civil War Battle of Bull Run. A 46-year-old school nurse took a cue from her students and called in sick to hear Obama speak.

And Wyman Robinson, a 62-year-old retired cop who drove from Maryland with his family to attend an Obama rally, said he was so confident that his man was bound for glory, he had already begun his quest for tickets to celebrate the Inauguration of Barack Obama as the 44th President of the United States in Washington on Tuesday, January 20, 2009.

Few Democrats shared Robinson's optimism. Only one Democrat, Bill Clinton, had served two full terms since World War II. History would have been different, many of its chroniclers and most Democrats believe, had not Al Gore's popular vote win in 2000 been hijacked in Florida and awarded to George W. Bush by the Supreme Court. The party's faithful were left in the aftermath feeling cheated and so snakebit that John Kerry's loss to Bush four years later seemed almost preordained.

Not even the resounding Democratic triumph in the midterm Congressional elections of 2006 was enough to dispel the hangover engendered by the past two presidential election defeats.

Compounding Democratic angst was the injection of race into the 2008 sweepstakes. Even the most seasoned and proven

Flanked by his wife, Michelle, daughters Malia and Sasha, and his running mate, Joe Biden and his wife, Jill, Obama had just finished delivering his acceptance speech at the Democratic Convention. "Tonight," he said, highlighting the economic theme that would lead him to the White House, "more Americans are out of work and more are working harder for less."

pollsters admitted that they could not predict the outcome in a showdown in which voters reluctant to admit racial bias might say they were voting for one candidate only to get in the booth and cast their ballot for the other.

Spurious so-called "whisper" campaigns played on deeply ingrained voter prejudices, alleging that Obama's biracial background made his loyalties suspect and that he was not a Christian, as he claimed, but was in fact "a Muslim who concealed his religion." Rumors that Obama was secretly "an Arab," that he attended Muslim schools as a child and was somehow involved in plots to overthrow the government went viral on the web.

At the same time, somewhat more subtle attacks used racially charged code words to cast Obama as "uppity" and "elitist" or "cooly arrogant," as Bush strategist turned FOX news analyst Karl Rove told a Republican breakfast gathering in June. "Even if you never met him," Rove said, "you know him. He's the guy at the country club with the beautiful date, holding a martini and a cigarette that stands against the wall and makes snide comments about everyone."

Many voters understood that Obama was a happily married man whose upbringing was a far cry from the country-club cloistered lives of privilege enjoyed in their youths by George W. Bush and John McCain; for them, Rove's comments, freighted with subliminal messages that played on class stereotypes and racial fears, ultimately backfired.

But there were those, particularly those in depressed regions enduring soaring unemployment and home mortgage foreclosures on top of sky-high fuel prices, who seemed to be swayed by appeals to prejudice.

"Most guys I know are for McCain and a lot of it's because of race," a West Virginia voter told a reporter. "Obama may be better for jobs. But a lot of us don't trust him."

"He's going to tear up the rose bushes and plant a watermelon patch," a man interviewed at a Wal-Mart store in Mobile, Alabama told a reporter. "I just don't think we'll ever have a black president."

Despite the fears of Obama supporters that Republican appeals to the demons rather than the better angels of the American psyche undermined their candidate's chances for victory in November, there was good reason to believe that the latest Democratic hope to lead his long out-of-power party back to the Pennsylvania Avenue Promised Land might succeed.

In spite of the long and bruising primary campaign, polls showed Obama with a small but solid lead over McCain. And his campaign's astonishing small donor fundraising success and grass roots organization skills allowed him to compete in once unassailable Republican strongholds.

The Democrats' so-called "50 state strategy" targeted safe Republican bets like Utah, which Bush had carried by huge margins. Instead of exhausting his campaign, the long primary fight, during which he created deep volunteer and fundraising organizations in all 50 states, actually strengthened Obama's plan to "expand the electoral map" and compete throughout the country.

With his economic message resonating among voters who were facing the highest gas prices ever seen in the U.S., where there were more unemployed workers, more families losing their homes and more living in poverty than most living Americans could remember, Obama turned his attention to foreign policy, considered to be McCain's strong suit and his own weakest.

"We continue to face grave threats, not only from terrorism, but also nuclear proliferation, climate change and poverty, genocide and disease," Obama said at the opening of a meeting of leading foreign affairs experts, including former secretaries of state Madeleine Albright and Warren Christopher, that he convened in Washington in late June.

In a *New York Times* op-ed piece published on the eve of a fact-finding visit to the Middle East, Obama said that, as president, he would "be as careful getting out of Iraq as we were careless getting in."

Throughout his subsequent tour of the Middle East, Obama, while officially a member of a congressional delegation, received the sort of greeting normally afforded a visiting head of state. In Afghanistan, he dined with troops ("the food was great, but the company was better," one American commander said after breakfasting with Barack) and met with the Afghan president, Hamid Karzai.

In Iraq, Obama met with Prime Minister Nouri al-Maliki and received a helicopter tour of Baghdad from Gen. David Petraeus, then top commander of American forces. After breakfasting with Israeli prime minister Ehud Olmert in Jerusalem, he conferred with Palestinian leaders in Ramallah, and received an especially warm greeting from the moderate Israeli president, Shimon Peres, who said he hoped the American people would elect a "great president of the United States. That is the greatest promise for us and the rest of the world."

Obama also made a favorable impression on hard-line Likud Party leader, Benjamin Netanyahu, who liked what his guest had to say about assuring Israel's security. Netanyahu told reporters that while the two men chatted casually, he asked his visitor

(Below) Obama talks with the top U.S. military commander in Iraq, David Petraeus, in a helicoptor over Baghdad on July 21. Iraq's government agreed with Obama on troop withdrawal goals, causing some embarrassment to the U.S. government, which had a different timetable.

how he was feeling. "I could fall asleep standing up," replied Obama.

After a year-and-a-half of near non-stop campaigning, Obama badly needed a break. He took one soon after he returned from his trip overseas. While visiting with his ailing grandmother, whose death was a heartbreaking moment in the closing days of the race, he relaxed with his wife and children in his native Hawaii. There, Obama worked on the speech that he would deliver in Denver in late August and fine-tuned his general election strategies.

Returning to the trail a week before the convention, Obama reminded a crowd in New Mexico that McCain's chief economic advisor, former congressman Phil Gramm, had recently downplayed the country's economic woes and said that the U.S. was "a nation of whiners."

"This guy obviously doesn't pump his own gas," Obama said, striking a theme that McCain and his economic advisors were out of touch with the problems facing ordinary Americans. "He obviously doesn't do his own shopping."

A week later, Obama was back where his campaign began 18 months earlier, in front of the Old State Capitol building in Springfield, Illinois. He introduced his running mate, one-time primary rival, Joe Biden of Delaware, hours after the news broke via text messages and e-mail sent to supporters by the hi-tech Obama campaign.

Though a disappointment to Hillary Clinton supporters, Biden, analysts pointed out, brought far less baggage, and far fewer negative voter impressions than the former first lady might have. And more importantly, Biden's age (65), his years of experience (his five-term career in the U.S. Senate began in 1973, when Obama was 12) and his foreign policy expertise (he is chairman of the Senate foreign relations committee), counter-balanced the very same deficits on the head of the ticket's resume.

Where Obama had repeatedly evoked the name of Abraham Lincoln in the "nation divided" speech that launched his campaign on a frigid day in February 2007, it was Biden's turn in the heat of the general election fight to conjure the name of Springfield's favorite son. "President Lincoln once instructed us to be sure to put your feet in the right place, then stand firm," Biden told the sweltering crowd of 20,000 who endured a hot, humid August afternoon in the plains to witness the historic event. "Today, Springfield, I know my feet are in the right place. And I am proud to stand firm for the next president—Barack Obama!"

As if to reaffirm his commitment to take the fight to the Republican heartland, Obama began his journey to the Democratic Convention in Denver with a "BBQ with Barack" event at the Eau Claire (Wisconsin) Rod and Gun Park. Refusing to cede to McCain an issue and voting block that had flummoxed Democrats for years, Obama used his appearance at the gun club to signal his readiness to find a fresh approach to solve conundrums that had long divided the electorate. "The reality of gun ownership," he would say a week later at the Democratic Convention, "may be different for hunters in rural Ohio than they are for those plagued by gang violence in Cleveland, but don't tell me we can't uphold the Second Amendment while keeping AK-47s out of the hands of criminals."

Obama would make his promise to "bridge divides" and "unite in common

As far as campaign surprises went, Obama's choice of Senator Joe Biden (pictured, second from left, with runner-up candidates Kansas Governor Kathleen Sebelius, left, Indiana Senator Evan Bayh and Virginia Governor Tim Kaine) paled next to the Sarah Palin shocker. But in the 65-year-old Biden, a Scranton native with a quarter century of service in the Senate, Obama found counterbalance to his own youth, perceived inexperience, and multi-cultural background.

effort" to solve polarizing problems ("We may not agree on abortion," he said, "but surely we can agree on reducing the number of unwanted pregnancies in this country"), a central theme of his nominating speech.

Delivered 45 years to the day after Martin Luther King, Jr. made his generation-defining "I Have a Dream" speech on the steps of the Lincoln Memorial, Obama's speech expressed in broad strokes and vivid, finely tuned detail, themes that he would return to again and again in the 40 days that remained before Election Day. His historic address—to date the most watched convention speech in history—had an audience of more than 40 million viewers who tuned in to see the first African American accept the nomination of a major political party.

With ratings that dwarfed even the season finale of *American Idol*, TV's most popular show, the prime time speech, delivered before a live audience of more than 70,000 in Denver's enormous Invesco Field football stadium, Obama's speech was praised by pundits across the political spectrum. It also seemed to give Obama the kind of momentum that had been missing from his campaign since he had clinched the nomination two months before.

Pleased as Democrats were with their nominee's showing in Denver, they seemed caught off-guard the following day when the morning news shows devoted their broadcasts not to the warm afterglow of their convention, but to astonishing news from the enemy camp.

On the heels of Obama's speech, John McCain made history himself on Friday, Aug. 29, his 72nd birthday, by tapping the utterly unknown former mayor of the tiny suburban town of Wasilla, Alaska, as his running mate. Not only had he named Sarah Palin as the first ever female Republican vice-presidential nominee, he had celebrated his birthday by hijacking the news cycle for the foreseeable future.

While Democrats smelled cynicism when Palin, a socially conservative, evangelical Christian who disagreed with Hillary Clinton on virtually every major issue, urged the failed Democratic candidate's supporters to rally to her banner, conservative Republicans rejoiced. "They're beyond ecstatic," said rightist Christian Coalition founder Ralph Reed. However, Democratic leader Rahm Emanuel said that McCain's choice was not only cynical, but dangerous. "On his 72nd birthday, this is the guy's judgment of who he wants one heartbeat from the presidency? Please."

By Monday, fears among his own supporters that McCain had goofed intensified dramatically when it was revealed that Palin's 17-year-old, unwed daughter was pregnant and that Palin herself was under investigation in her home state for abusing her powers as governor. (True to his word that he would not stoop to personal attacks, Obama issued a statement supporting the Palin family's right to privacy and admonished his campaign staff to make no comments about the teenager's pregnancy.)

Palin managed to silence critics at least temporarily with a resounding convention speech that electrified Republicans and enthralled an enormous television audience that surpassed the one that had tuned in for Obama's now overshadowed speech five days before. Palin introduced herself ("just your average hockey mom"), her family (including her two intriguingly named sons, Track, an Iraq bound teen, and Trig, a 4-month old with Down syndrome, as well as the pregnant Bristol) and a few choice phrases to the lexicon. "[A] small town mayor is sort of like a . . .'community organizer,' except that you have actual responsibilities," she said in mocking reference to Obama.

Quickly, however, the gloss was off. Within weeks, thanks to her thin

(Left) During his acceptance speech, Obama predicted that McCain would attack his patriotism rather than debate the issues. "The men and women who serve in our battlefields may be Democrats and Republicans and independents, but they have fought together, and bled together, and some died together under the same proud flag." (Above) Sarah Palin (here, from left, with son Track, daughter Bristol and her boyfriend, Levi Johnston, daughters Willow and Piper, husband Todd and, in her arms, baby Trig) electrified the Republican Convention, which had been delayed by Hurricane Gustav. But not all party members applauded McCain's choice. "We're in a global war," said one mystified delegate from Alabama, "so it's less than honest if someone says that this woman is qualified to lead America right now." (Right) Republican insiders said that McCain (with Palin following his acceptance speech at the GOP convention in St. Paul, Minnesota) hoped to name Joe Leiberman as his running mate. Under pressure from conservatives, advisers rejected him because of his pro-choice views. Palin was chosen days before the convention. "This was really kind of rushed," a GOP insider said of the Palin choice, "because John didn't get what he wanted."

resume—the former mayor of Wasilla, with a population of 7,000, had served as governor of the Alaska for 20 months—and feeble performance in a series of interviews, most notably with Katie Couric, Palin proved a liability to the campaign.

Palin managed to avoid disaster in her much anticipated October 2 debate with Joe Biden, and continued to draw large and enthusiastic crowds of fired up Republicans on the campaign trail. However she would be embarrassed by the results of an investigation by the Alaska Legislature, released October 10, that concluded that she had abused her powers as governor.

Palin's support among independent, undecided, and uncommitted Democratic voters, as well as surprising numbers of Republicans, plummeted in polls. The McCain campaign also appeared to founder in the wake of the financial meltdown that had already engulfed Wall Street, causing bank failures, the collapse of major investment firms, as well as threatening the stock holdings of Main Street's millions of small investors. The crisis made the shortcomings of his running mate all the more glaring.

On September 24, McCain announced that he was going to suspend his campaign so that he could go to Washington and participate in negotiations over the administration's $700 billion Wall Street bailout plan and called for a postponement of the first presidential debate, scheduled to be held two days later. Obama joined McCain in calling for passage of the bailout plan but strongly urged that the debate go on. "This is exactly the time when the American people need to hear from the person who will be the next president," he said while campaigning in Florida. "It is going to be part of the president's job to deal with more than one thing at once."

Suddenly it was Obama, not his multitask-adverse elder, who struck the statesmanlike tone, ticking off a series of provisions to improve the bailout measure, while McCain's suspension of his campaign seemed erratic and, said New York Senator Chuck Schumer, "just weird."

Two days later, McCain decided to participate in the debate after all. Planned as a discussion about foreign policy, moderator Jim Lehrer asked the candidates to also address the economy. Saddled by his support for the unpopular and treasure-draining war in Iraq and Republican "trickle down" economic policies, McCain seemed off-balance throughout. When Obama faulted his opponent's judgment for cheerleading the Iraq invasion, McCain continued to do so, claiming that "victory" was at hand.

Following the candidates' second debate, on October 7, in Nashville, Tennessee, polls showed that Obama was beginning to pull ahead of McCain, whose Palin-fuelled post-convention boost had evaporated in the heat of the economic crisis.

With an overwhelming number of voters agreeing that the economy was the number one issue facing the nation and that Obama was best suited for dealing with it, the McCain campaign went negative.

"That's to be expected," Obama had said in his acceptance speech, predicting that his opponent would go on the attack, "because if you don't have any fresh ideas, then you use stale tactics to scare voters."

McCain did just that. On the stump and in the candidates' final debate on October 15, the Republican painted Obama as a tax-and-spend liberal but also as a "socialist" who embraced the "tenets of Marxism." He also claimed Obama had a sinister association with former sixties radical William Ayers, a Chicago educator and neighbor of Obama's who had been prosecuted for his violent opposition to the Vietnam War when the candidate was a child living with his grandparents in Hawaii. McCain hoped these attacks would cause voters to question Obama's patriotism and his fitness for office. Most pollsters would later agree that the negative attacks hurt the GOP candidate more than their intended target.

The most odd and unexpected moment in a long campaign already known for its surprises, occurred in the final debate when the American people were introduced to one Samuel J. Wurzelbacher. Immortalized by John McCain as Joe the Plumber, Wurzelbacher, a bald and burly conservative independent from Holland, Ohio, had approached Obama on Sunday, October 12, as he made a surprise campaign stop on the eve of the debate. Renowned as he was for inspiring stadium-size audiences with his oratory, Obama was engaging in old-fashioned campaigning in Holland, knocking on doors and introducing himself to the locals. As word spread that Barack was on the block, dozens of residents flocked to see the candidate.

Among the crowd was Wurzelbacher who shouted: "Do you believe in the American dream?" When Obama said that he did indeed, Wurzelbacher complained about his taxes. "I'm getting ready to buy a company that makes $250,000 to $280,000 a year," Wurzelbacher said. "Your new tax plan is going to tax me more, isn't it?"

After first explaining that he intended to reduce taxes for the overwhelming majority of Americans, Obama admitted that yes, someone earning as much as Wurzelbacher claimed would face an increase.

"I think that when you spread the wealth around, it's good for everybody," Obama added, uttering the phrase that would be repeated again and again by his rivals. The candidate had no way of knowing that the

"In the final days of campaigns, the say-anything, do-anything politics too often takes over. We've seen it before. And we're seeing it again today."

BARACK OBAMA

After Obama and McCain faced off in their third and final debate on October 15, an independent voter from Missouri described Obama as being "level headed, calm, cool and collected under pressure." McCain by contrast struck the same voter as being a "hothead. . . I don't feel he's very stable mentally," he said.

exchange would wind up first on YouTube, then *FOX News*, thrusting Wurzelbacher to the campaign's center stage and handing McCain fresh ammo for an intensified attack strategy.

After hailing "Joe the Plumber" by name nine times during the October 14 debate, McCain made him the centerpiece of his campaign's closing argument. He cast Wurzelbacher as a kind of one-man truth squad who was able to crack Obama's cool façade and expose the feared "socialist" boogeyman within. McCain invited Wurzelbacher to join him on stage at campaign rallies, praised him even when he didn't show up, and promised to take the plumber to Washington in January to help, McCain said, "drain the swamp."

(Left) The focus of numerous attacks on Obama, former sixties radical William Ayers (in 1980) lived three blocks from Obama's home in Hyde Park, on the Southside of Chicago. "It seems manifestly unfair to tarnish him with this association," said the retired prosecutor who led the trial against Ayers in the early 1970s. "Obama knew Ayers during a period he was named Citizen of the Year in Chicago, not when he was committing those terrorist acts." (Above) When Obama chatted with Samuel "Joe the Plumber" Wurzelbacher while campaigning in Holland, Ohio, on October 12, McCain used the exchange to accuse his opponent of waging "class warfare." Democrats, he said, would "take Joe's money, give it to Senator Obama and let him spread the wealth around." "It's pretty surreal," Wuzelbacher said of his 15 minutes in the spotlight.

Polls would show that the attacks backfired and that most voters recognized the socialist tag that McCain hung on Obama in the closing weeks of the campaign was no more credible than Wurzelbacher's credentials. Joe was indeed a plumber, but not a licensed one, and though he was certainly an angry taxpayer, he had not actually paid all of the taxes that he complained about owing.

And yet, McCain's campaign continued to bludgeon his opponent with the patently false charge that he was a socialist bent on taxing America to death, right up to the eve of the election. He also took every opportunity to exploit Obama's non-existent present-day ties to William Ayers and made no real effort to tone down Sarah Palin's anger-inciting rhetoric about Obama "palling around with terrorists" (attacks that led both the Republican statesman Colin Powell and the conservative icon Christopher Buckley to endorse Obama).

In the end, Joe the Plumber was not destined for a role in a new McCain administration. Like Joe Six-pack, the fictional everyman who had earlier been conjured to broaden the Republican's appeal among the economically hard-hit working class, Wurzelbacher became no more than a footnote in one of the most momentous and profound chapters in American history.

The magnitude of the historic force that would end Republican residency in the White House and expand Democratic control of Congress was glimpsed as Election Day dawned on Tuesday, November 4. Thousands of voters lined up to cast their ballots hours before polling places opened. Although opinion polls had found that Obama had actually widened his lead on the eve of the election, the day when a trailing candidate typically closes the gap, it was nonetheless a day of high anxiety for most Democrats. There was widespread talk of the so-called "Bradley effect," named for the black mayor of Los Angeles, Tom Bradley, who lost a re-election bid despite having enjoyed a healthy lead in the polls. Many Obama supporters feared that no matter what potential voters told pollsters, whites would never vote for an African-American candidate for president.

And yet, it was that impossible dream that compelled unprecedented millions of black voters to go to the polls and cast their ballots for Barack Obama. Among them was the Reverend Horace C. Boyd, an 81-year-old pastor from Georgia who said that until 1961, the year Obama was born, he was not allowed to vote in any local or national election. At a time when only 100 of the 20,000 blacks who lived in his county were able to vote, white election officials used so-called "literacy tests" to exclude blacks. Boyd told the *New York Times*'s Kevin Sack that he vividly recalled the sense of humiliation and powerlessness he felt when he was barred from voting for being unable to answer the absurd question "how many bubbles were in a bar of soap."

Stirring stories circulated of massive, record-breaking voter turn outs throughout the nation, a sign that boded well for Obama. However, many Democrats continued to fear the worst.

One Democratic organizer said he sensed a change in North Carolina when he passed a white driver in a pick-up truck with a gun rack mounted in the rear window—a typical McCain supporter—and was surprised to see that its door was plastered with Obama decals.

"I thought, 'We might be winning [this election],' the organizer said. "In difficult times, people find the price of prejudice is a bit too high. They're saying 'We don't care what your race is. If you can make things better, we're for you.'"

Returns came in as a trickle at first, with Obama declared the winner in Vermont and McCain in the early electoral college lead thanks to his win in Kentucky. But as the first of the large battleground states like Pennsylvania and Ohio and Florida were scored for Obama, and word spread on the Internet that huge voter turnouts nationwide guaranteed a Democratic landslide, supporters began to believe that the outcome that seemed impossible two years earlier had actually occurred.

Fittingly, in a race in which brilliant use of the Internet helped his campaign build a world-class political organization and fund-raising apparatus, Obama's dramatic win was first projected not by the major broadcast and cable news networks, but by upstart political Web sites.

With the traditional election news sources reluctant to cite exit polls prematurely or to project winners while voters were still casting ballots, on-line blogs like *Slate*, the *Huffington Post* and *Time* magazine's *The Page*, declared Obama the winner 90 minutes before television viewers learned the news at 11 p.m. By the time the networks made it official, John McCain and George W. Bush had already telephoned their congratulations to the 44th President-in-waiting.

"An African-American has broken the barrier as old as the Republic," announced NBC's Brian Williams.

In small gatherings and large, the news triggered emotions that ran the gamut from lingering disbelief and wonderment to unbridled joy. Exultant crowds filled Times Square in New York and Grant Park in Chicago where celebrated figures like Oprah Winfrey and Jesse Jackson stood tearfully among the crush of thousands to witness Obama's first public appearance as President-Elect.

Obama's historic achievement stirred deep, cathartic emotions. "It brought tears to my eyes," said a maintenance man in Atlanta, who was among many who sensed that a long promised dream had finally been fulfilled. "Everything that Martin Luther King talked about is coming true."

Whether viewed as Martin Luther King, Jr.'s dream realized, the fulfillment of Lincoln's own promised "new burst of freedom," or, as one of Obama's legions of new-generation supporters called the spontaneous celebrations, "our own Woodstock," it certainly seemed, as syndicated columnist Thomas Friedman noted the next day, that Barack Obama had already delivered on his promise of change. "[W]e awake this morning to a different country," Friedman wrote, echoing the call for hope that the President-Elect had made throughout his campaign. "Let every child and every citizen and every new immigrant know that from this day forward, everything really is possible in America."

(Far left) Once again echoing Lincoln, as he had done since launching his long-shot campaign nearly two years earlier, Obama (celebrating his victory with Vice President-Elect Joe Biden in Grant Park) said that voters "proved that more than two centuries later, a government of the people, by the people, and for the people has not perished from the Earth." (Top left) "I would not be standing here tonight without the unyielding support of my best friend for the last sixteen years, the rock of our family, the love of my life, the nation's next first lady, Michelle Obama," the man who will be inaugurated Jan. 20, 2009, as the 44th President said in an elegant victory speech. (Bottom left) "The American people have spoken, and they have spoken clearly," John McCain, with his wife Cindy and running mate Sarah Palin and her husband Todd looking on, said in a gracious concession speech in which he congratulated Obama "on being elected the next president of the country that we both love." (Above) "If there is anyone out there who still doubts that America is a place where all things are possible...tonight is your answer," Obama told the jubilant crowd on election night. He garnered at least 365 electoral votes, more than double those received by McCain, and won the battleground states of Florida, Indiana, North Carolina, and Ohio, to become the first African American president. "It's been a long time coming, but tonight, because of what we did on this day, in this election, at this defining moment, change has come to America."

PRESIDENT BARACK OBAMA

8

Barack Obama's earliest supporters had a ready explanation for why countless numbers of ordinary citizens like themselves abandoned all reason and devoted themselves heart and soul to his candidacy. They had become drunk, they said, on "Obama Juice," the heady elixir that made them believe that the black man with the funny name might actually succeed in his seemingly absurd quest to be elected president of the United States of America. When the dream came true, it seemed like the entire nation was tipsy from the Obama high.

Joining the euphoric chorus hailing Obama's victory were even a few famously teetotaling occupants of the White House. "It will be a stirring sight to watch President

All The Men Presidents: For the first time since 1981, the living past, present, and future Chief Executives met in the Oval Office on January 7 (center). "One message that I have, and I think we all share, is that we want you to succeed," the sitting president told the president-elect before they joined George H. W. Bush (left), Bill Clinton and Jimmy Carter for lunch and table talk. "Whether we're Democrat or Republican, we care deeply about this country." Said Obama, who suggested the meeting during his first post-election visit to the White House in November: "All the gentlemen here understand both the pressures and possibilities of this office. And for me to have the opportunity to get advice, good counsel, and fellowship with these individuals is extraordinary. And I'm very grateful to all of them." While the incoming and outgoing presidents bonded during the transition, Obama (strolling with Bush in the White House Colonnade, top, and meeting in the Oval Office, left, during his November 10 visit) was expected to undo many of his predecessor's policies. Intending to lift bans on family planning and stem cell research, Obama also planned to end Bush's policies of selling public lands to for-profit, private interests and putting big business lobbyists for timber, energy, and finance companies, among others, in charge of the very agencies that were meant to regulate them.

After years of high tension between the Republicans in the White House and Democrats in Congress, Obama met with Speaker of the House Nancy Pelosi on January 5 (top), signaling a new era of cooperation between the branches. Calling for "dramatic action" to tackle a "crisis unlike any we have seen in our lifetime," Obama and Vice President-elect Joe Biden met that same day with Senate majority leader Harry Reid and leaders from both parties (above) in his on-going efforts to build congressional support for an emergency spending bill to jump start the economy.

Obama, his wife, Michelle, and their beautiful girls step through the doors of the White House," said the Democrats' nemesis in chief, George W. Bush.

"As an African American, I am especially proud," outgoing Secretary of State Condoleezza Rice said the day after Obama's historic win. "Yesterday was obviously an extraordinary step forward."

"Who among us is not at a loss for words?" iconoclastic filmmaker Michael Moore wrote in a blog post to fans accustomed to him throwing brickbats not hosannas. "Tears pour out. Tears of joy. Tears of relief. A stunning, whopping landslide of hope in a time of deep despair."

Writers rhapsodized about what *People* magazine's Bill Hewitt termed Obama's "astonishing" political ascent. Hewitt adds, "The brown-skinned son of a white mother from Kansas and a black father from Kenya, one who lived for a time in Indonesia (eating tiger meat!) and tried cocaine as a teen in Hawaii, he presented some stunningly original growth rings for presidential timber."

Even as Obama supporters partied till dawn, celebrating what the *New York Times* called "a new era in a country where just 143 years ago, Mr. Obama, as a black man, could have been owned as a slave," the president-elect cancelled a planned fireworks display after his Grant Park victory party in order to remind the nation that his election came at a time of war and grave economic crisis. Instead of celebrating into the wee hours, he left the champagne on ice and returned with his family to his Hyde Park home. He was determined, aides said, to get up early the next morning, see his daughters off to school, and then get down to the nation's business.

And little of it was going to be pleasant. Once inaugurated, *Time* magazine noted, Obama would face "the toughest first year [in the White House] since Franklin Roosevelt's." In fact, the new president would need to tackle even more fearsome crises than those that loomed before FDR at his first inauguration seventy-five years earlier.

Roosevelt took power when the nation was bogged down in the Great Depression. However, unlike President Obama, the thirty-second president did not have to fight two wars raging in the planet's most dangerous subcontinent or contend with threats at home from terrorists eager to arm themselves with pirated nuclear weapons or respond to urgent warnings of pending worldwide environmental disaster, all while struggling to solve the worst economic crisis of his lifetime.

Even the seventy-seven-day transition period on which Obama embarked November 5 was itself perilous. Until his swearing in on January 20, 2009, when he would take the reins of power from his lame-duck predecessor in the first such presidential handover since terrorists attacked the United States nine months into Bush's first term, the leadership of the most powerful democracy on Earth would remain in limbo.

To minimize the danger—and at the risk of being accused of prematurely measuring drapes in the White House months before a vote was cast in the general election—Obama assigned Bill Clinton's former chief of staff John Podesta to prepare for a transition to an Obama administration. "I was absolutely convinced... that, whether it was me or John McCain, the next president-elect was going to have to move swiftly," Obama told *Time*. And so, long before election night, the FBI, at Podesta's prodding, had already screened likely candidates to fill key positions in the would-be president's cabinet and staff.

Feeling it was urgent to make good on his promise to hit the ground running if elected, Obama barely paused to savor his victory. Having notched what will be remembered as one of the most astounding political triumphs in American history and surely exhausted by the nonstop, two-year effort, the forty-fourth president-to-be refused to take the day off. After rising early the morning after the election and having breakfast with his wife and children, Obama went to work at his transition offices in downtown Chicago. Instead of parsing the election results and exulting in victory, he convened and chaired a five-hour meeting of his staff to draw up a short list of White House staff and cabinet appointees and to map out a strategy for his first hundred days in office.

"He feels like he has a real mandate for change," transition chief Podesta told reporters, reiterating the incoming president's urgent desire to move swiftly to fix what was broken in Washington. "We need to get off the course that the Bush administration has set."

That the torch of American leadership had been passed to a new generation was quickly underscored when it was announced that the president-elect—who listened to Fugees tunes on his iPod, was seldom seen without his BlackBerry and cell phone close at hand during the campaign, and had posted photos from the election-night celebration in Grant Park on Flickr—insisted that his first radio address to the nation be made simultaneously available for viewing on YouTube.

"Oh, wow!" Obama said, sounding like a member of the youth movement that helped elect him, when he arrived for a press conference at the Chicago Hilton on Friday, November 7. That muted exclamation was as close as he came to expressing amazement at the enormity of his accomplishment and the bewildering speed of his political rise: according to polls, Obama's name, utterly unknown in November 2000, when his predecessor won his first term in office, was still a mystery to most Americans in 2006, when he began contemplating his own White House run; now, just two years later, he was standing at a podium emblazoned with the seal of the Office of the President-Elect.

Leaving the whiplash to others, Obama immediately turned to the business at hand. "I do not underestimate the enormity of the task that lies ahead," he said as he introduced his team of economic advisors and adopted the can-do tone that would lead *Time* to describe him as "a Mr. Fix It going to Washington." Continued Obama, "It is not going to be quick and it is not going to be easy for us to dig ourselves out of the hole that we are in."

After enumerating the dire dimensions of the abyss, including some three million auto industry jobs at risk and an economy on the tipping point from recession to depression, the president-elect turned to a more lighthearted topic. Obama spoke of how he promised his daughters, Malia and Sasha, a puppy, preferably a nonshedding one (Malia has asthma and is allergic) from a pet shelter, as a reward for having endured Daddy's absence from home for most of the past two years. "Obviously," he said in a memorably disarming phrase, "a lot of shelter dogs are mutts like me."

And from that shaggy-dog moment, the inevitable spin began. Before the day was out, Fox News commentators were setting the soon-to-be First Dad up for a hit, illustrating their coverage of the future White House puppy with photos of dangerous-looking dogs behind bars. With one shot of a shelter-incarcerated pit bull displayed on the screen behind them, Fox's talking heads seemed to suggest that Obama was willing to endanger his family in order to do the politically correct thing.

Taking a similarly sly tact after it was reported a few days later that the Obamas were considering sending their daughters to a private school in Washington, conservative columnist Cal Thomas attempted to pin the president-elect on the twin horns of another dilemma: should Obama "pander to the teachers unions" and send his daughters to one of Washington DC's "miserable public schools" or send them to an elitist private school? It was a choice, Thomas wrote, denied "every other American who cannot afford to pay private school tuition."

A less mischievous but more provocative reaction to Obama's win was reported in Greenville, South Carolina, where a Catholic priest told his parishioners they were not welcome to receive communion if they voted for Obama, whose pro-choice belief, the priest said, "constitutes material cooperation with intrinsic evil."

The same priest had nothing to say about reports by law enforcement and human rights groups around the country of a sharp uptick in threats, racial slurs, and actual violence directed at Obama and his supporters. Racial incidents from cross burnings and Obama-in-effigy lynchings to racially motivated vandalism, school-yard taunts, and classroom intimidation were reported from coast to coast.

"Someone once said racism is like cancer," noted a University of North Carolina expert in race relations. "It's never totally wiped out; it's in remission." Sadly, despite the progress so dramatically proved by Obama's election, the disease remained virulent in the land.

That life had changed forever for Obama and his family was clear from the moment the president-elect awoke on November 5 and found himself insulated inside the bubble that will encase him until the day he leaves the White House, be it four or eight Januaries in the future.

Entrusted with the safety of the commander in chief and his family, the Secret Service, with assists from the Chicago Police Department, saw to it that the streets around the family's Hyde Park home were closed to all outside traffic throughout the transition period. Concrete barriers that surrounded the candidate's home during the campaign were moved three blocks out on the day after the election, and ID cards were issued to all residents, frequent guests, and employees of neighborhood homes and businesses, as well as the two-thousand-member congregation of a nearby synagogue. "It's a little inconvenient," said one neighbor. "I don't mind, though, because I got the president I voted for."

Obama (Secret Service code name Renegade) was told that he could no longer tool around in his private automobile (he would be chauffeured to and from home in an armored limo with a motorcycle escort) or stroll the neighborhood and drop in as he pleased at his favorite pastry shop (Medici), bookstore (57th Street Books), or lunch spot (Valois). When he wanted to take his wife out for a romantic meal at the couple's

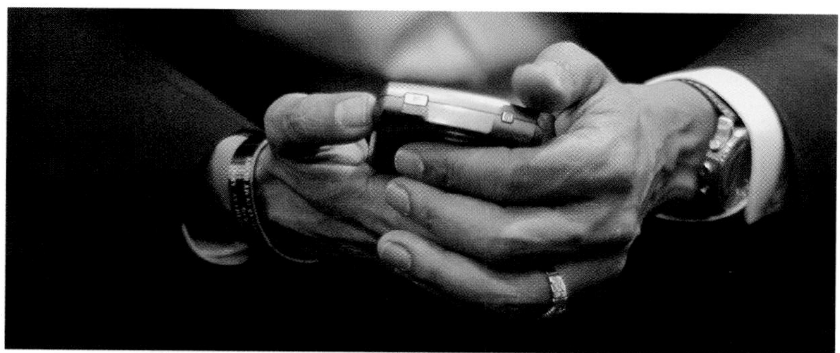

The transition had its pains as well as its pleasures for Obama. "I'm still clinging to my BlackBerry," the president-elect (texting in St. Louis last summer, top) said of his strong desire to keep the device after he takes office and becomes the nation's first wired chief executive. Government policy dictates that for security reasons, the president cannot use his own gadget. "They're going to pry it out of my hands." Marketing experts said that Obama's product endorsement would earn him as much as $50 million if he were a private citizen. But the president-elect (teeing off December 29 at a private golf course in Kailua, Hawaii, above) was able to unwind during his two-week Christmas holiday on the island of Oahu, where he was born. "It doesn't seem to have changed him at all," said a friend. "He's the same relaxed, in control, engaging Barack that he's always been. [His election] hasn't shifted him at all."

favorite Italian restaurant in downtown Chicago, Spiaggia, as he did on the Saturday night following the election, he had company. "It's always just the two of them," the lakefront restaurant's chef said of past visits by the Obamas. "Now it's just the two of them and thirty Secret Service agents."

Obama also found that, when in need of a haircut, he could no longer get a trim at the same Hyde Park barbershop he'd been going to for the past fourteen years. From now on, the Secret Service insisted, Obama's barber would have to administer his usual twenty-one-dollar clip job in the secure confines of the Regents Park gym where the president-elect worked out every day. "He walks a little different," Obama's barber told the *New York Times* after a recent session with his famous customer. "He's looking a lot more presidential now."

"There was an unfamiliar sound," commented a newsman covering Barack and Michelle Obama's first postelection trip to Washington for a visit with the outgoing First Family on November 10: "Cheering outside the White House gates." And there would soon be new sounds from within as well: the voices and laughter of Malia, ten, and Sasha, seven, the youngest children to occupy the White House since Amy Carter, who was nine when her father was inaugurated in 1977. "This will be even more of a transition for the girls," Michelle Obama said of the election's impact on her daughters. For them the new president's mandate for change meant moving out of the only home they'd known to a big new house in a strange city where they would soon start new lives at a new school and, they hoped, make new friends.

"Our concern," Michelle told *People*, "is that they stay normal." To that end, Obama attended a parent-teacher conference at the girls' Chicago school days after his election, and the families of the girls' friends promised to stay in close touch. "We are all going to help Sasha and Malia keep their

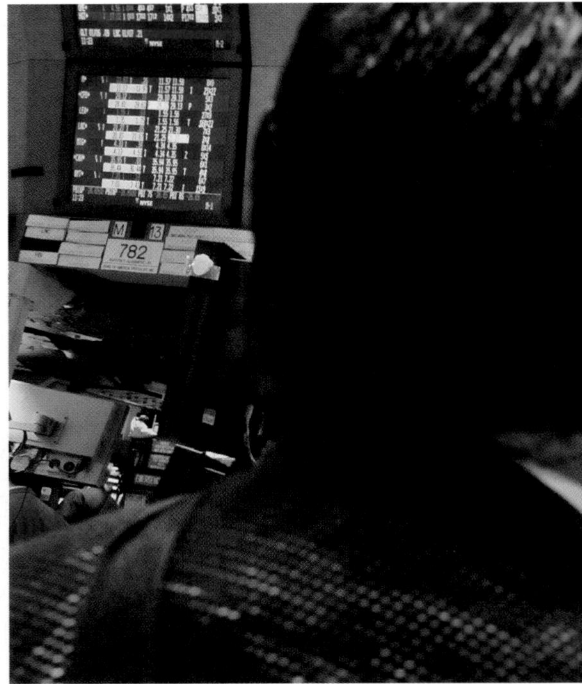

lives as normal as possible," said the father of one of the girls' best friends. "We have a strong family community that will more than cover the distance between [Chicago] and Washington."

Once in Washington, Michelle said, she has no plans to involve herself in the workings of government as Hillary Clinton did during her tenancy in the White House. "My first job," the future First Lady told *Ebony* magazine, "is going to be mom in chief." Her priority, she said, was to get the girls settled in their new home and to be sure "that they know they will continue to be the center of our universe."

Before setting off on her own to inspect area schools for the children during the Obamas' November visit—they eventually settled on the Sidwell Friends School, where Malia and Sasha began classes January 5—Michelle was given a tour of the White House's family quarters while her husband and the outgoing president talked policy downstairs. ("It's a really nice office," Obama quipped to his press secretary, Robert Gibbs, after meeting with Bush in the president's famous Oval Office.

With their living quarters taking up thirty-three rooms on the second and third floors of the mansion at 1600 Pennsylvania Avenue, Malia (Secret Service code name Radiance) and Sasha (Rosebud) will have lots of exploring to do—when they are not busy practicing their serves on the enclosed, year-round tennis court, bowling on the White House lanes, taking lessons on the second-floor grand piano, munching goodies in the well-stocked pastry shop, or digging into the popcorn cart at the executive mansion movie theater.

Determined to disrupt the children's routine as little as possible, the Obamas allowed Malia and Sasha to finish the semester at their Chicago school before the family headed to Hawaii for a long-delayed holiday. During a two-week Christmas vacation

Scenes from the transition (from far left): It was up in the morning and off to school for the soon-to-be first daughters Sasha (left) and Malia, who got a send-off from mom and dad on their first day at the Sidwell Friends School on Monday, January 5. The Obamas, who arrived in Washington early so that the girls could start the semester with their new classmates, stayed at the Capitol's historic Hay Adams Hotel until the official president-elect's residence became available on January 15. Traders at the New York Stock Exchange (right) watched Obama give his January 8 speech at Virginia's George Mason University in which he excoriated Wall Street executives for making "imprudent and dangerous decisions, seeking profits with too little regard for risk, too little regulatory scrutiny, and too little accountability."

spent beachcombing and bodysurfing on the island of Oahu, where their father was born, the girls visited the Honolulu Zoo with the president-elect and then gathered with relatives, including Obama's half sister Maya Soetoro-Ng, for a memorial service for his maternal grandmother, Madelyn Dunham, who died on the eve of Obama's election—but not before casting an absentee ballot for her grandson.

Packing their bags and flying back to Chicago on New Year's Day, the Obamas spent the holiday weekend going about the bittersweet business of moving. The girls, due to start classes on Monday, January 5, flew with their mom to Washington on Saturday while the president-elect stayed behind to close his transition offices and spend one last night in the family house in Hyde Park.

The next morning, as he boarded a presidential jet to Washington, Obama told reporters that he "choked up a little bit" as he locked up the house for the last time. A friend of Malia's had stopped by and left a photo album full of pictures of the girls growing up together as a going-away present. "I just looked through the pages," he said. "The house was empty. It was a little tough. It got me."

By the time he landed in Washington, Obama had announced most of his major cabinet nominees, including, among the most prominent, secretary of state designate Hillary Clinton, the onetime Democratic front-runner whose apparent lock on the nomination was thwarted by her new boss, and Robert M. Gates, the Bush appointee who took over the Department of Defense after Donald Rumsfeld was forced from office following the 2006 midterm elections. With their nominations—as well as that of New Mexico governor and former Democratic presidential candidate Bill Richardson, who withdrew his nomination as commerce secretary when it was revealed that he was the subject of a federal investigation—Obama appeared to be taking yet another cue from Lincoln, the president whose memory he had evoked at every turn since announcing his candidacy in the rail-splitter's hometown of Springfield, Illinois, two years before.

Citing Doris Kearns Goodwin's *Team of Rivals*, her book about the leadership style of Lincoln, Obama explained his decisions to appoint Clinton and Richardson, to reach across the aisle to choose Gates, and to seek audiences with McCain and Bush in his efforts to unite the country and solve the enormous problems it faced. "Lincoln," Obama said, "basically pulled . . . all the people who had been running against him into his cabinet because whatever personal feelings there were, the issue was: How can we get this country through this time of crisis?"

There were bumps in the road during the closing weeks of his transition—hard on the heels of Richardson's withdrawal, Democrats and Republicans alike expressed displeasure at Obama's appointment of an intelligence community outsider, Leon Panetta, as head of the CIA, and some conservative Democrats joined Republicans in expressing distress over the details of Obama's plan to jump-start the economy with a spending program that would make the already record budget deficit far greater. However, the president-elect garnered far more praise than criticism. "As Obama has moved with unprecedented speed to build an administration that would bolster the confidence of a shaken world, his flash and dazzle have faded into the background," wrote *Time*'s David Von Drehle in naming Obama the magazine's Person of the Year. "In the waning days of his extraordinary year and on the cusp of his presidency, what now seems most salient about Obama is the opposite of flashy, the antithesis of rhetoric: he gets things done."

Obama's nominee for secretary of state, Hillary Clinton, promised that that under her leadership "the State Department will be firing on all cylinders to provide forward-looking, sustained diplomacy in every part of the world." Clinton testified on Capitol Hill January 13 (above left) before the Senate Foreign Relations Committee chaired by John Kerry, the former presidential candidate who first boosted Obama to national prominence by tapping him to speak at the 2004 Democratic convention. (Right) With Lincoln having loomed large in Obama's campaign from the beginning, the 44th president-elect kicked off the opening inaugural celebration at the 16th's memorial on January 18. Obama, who would be sworn in on January 20, 2009, the bicentennial year of Lincoln's birth, chose an inaugural theme that echoes the Gettysburg Address: "A New Birth of Freedom."

On the eve of his inauguration as the 44th President of the United States, Barack Obama rolled up the sleeves of his white shirt and helped paint the blue walls of a homeless shelter for teenage boys in downtown Washington, D.C. "Given the crisis that we're in and the hardships that so many people are going through, we can't allow any idle hands," Obama said as he encouraged Americans to participate in volunteer public service events on the Martin Luther King birthday holiday. "Everybody's got to be involved."

It was a theme that Obama struck throughout a three day walk-up to his inaugural that began with a symbolic ride by rail from Philadelphia to Washington on Saturday, January 17. Once again evoking the guiding spirit of his election campaign, Abraham Lincoln, who arrived from Illinois for his inauguration in 1861 by rail, Obama exhorted audiences "to do the hard work of perfecting our union."

Though he would take the oath of office with his hand resting on the same Bible that the 14th President used in his first inauguration, it was George Washington, whose trials in the winter of 1776 that Barack Hussein Obama dramatically recalled in his own inaugural address. "In the year of America's birth, in the coldest of months," he said, "a small band of patriots huddled by nine campfires on the shores of an icy river. The capital was abandoned. The enemy was advancing. The snow was stained with blood."

Things weren't quite that dire 233 years later. But Americans were once again "facing common dangers, in our winter of hardships" and the 44th president was taking office, he reminded the nation, "amidst gathering clouds and raging storms."

Throughout his speech, Obama evoked the darkest passages of American history even as he embodied its brightest promise. Standing on the steps of the Capitol, a building constructed by slaves, the nation's first black president addressed an emotional crowd of nearly two million people gathered on the National Mall, once the site of a slave market, that stretched more than a mile to the Washington monument, a memorial to the nation's first president, himself a slave-owner. "[W]e have endured the lash of the whip," he said. "[W]e have tasted the bitter swill of civil war and segregation and emerged from that dark chapter stronger and more united."

And it was America's promise of liberty for all, said Obama, the son of a black African, that drew those multitudes to "this magnificent mall." And it was "why a man whose father less than 60 years ago might not have been served at a local restaurant can now stand before you to take a most sacred oath."

For all the minor key themes Obama struck in his speech, the tears shed by the gathered witnesses to his historic inauguration expressed joy. And lest there be any doubt that Obama was up for the task of leading the nation as we "brave once more the icy currents" that Washington endured as he crossed the Delaware to pave the way for the nation's birth, the new president's characteristic grace and aplomb was evident throughout a long and no doubt trying Inaugural day that began with a workout at dawn at the president-elect's residence and ended in the White House after midnight.

When Chief Justice Roberts mangled the oath, Obama smiled and waited patiently for him to get it right. When Ted Kennedy was fell ill during a Congressional lunch, the newly sworn leader of the free world came to his aide. Whether dancing with his wife in the parade review stand or together with his daughters flashing the Aloha spirit "shaka" hand sign as his Punahou high school alma mater marching band rocked Pennsylvania Avenue, the 44th president displayed his renowned "No Drama Obama" cool.

In Swahili, Obama's father's language, Barack means "blessing." In Hebrew, Obama has said, it means "flash of lightening."

Whether Obama will achieve greatness and prove himself to be remembered, like Washington and Lincoln and FDR, as a blessing to his nation and one of the truly great presidents, or a single-term bolt from the blue, whose stirring election victory lighted the skies momentarily, the first African-American president's place in history is indelible.

"There was something very private and almost personal about being here," said one member of the enormous crowd that witnessed the inauguration of the first black president (top). Among the flag waving, "Obama!" chanting multitude was a man carrying a sign that read: "We Have Overcome!" (Right) While the new president and vice-president and their wives waved respectfully to the departing former president, members of their staffs gave Bush Bronx cheers. Some sang a mocking version of Steam's arena anthem: "Nah nah, hey hey, good bye!" (Bottom right) Obama and Michelle lead the parade down Pennsylvania Avenue to the White House. "This is a huge civil rights moment," the Rev. Jesse Jackson said of the Inauguration that took place the day after birthday observances for Martin Luther King. "Barack Obama has run the last lap of a [half-century] race for civil rights." (Bottom) "I have the special honor of being the guy who accompanied Michelle Obama to the ball," the President said of the new First Lady, who wore an ivory gown by Jason Wu, as they danced at the Commander in Chief Inaugural Ball, one of ten black tie affairs the couple attended.

President Barack Obama's Inaugural Address, Jan. 20, 2009

My fellow citizens:

I stand here today humbled by the task before us, grateful for the trust you have bestowed, mindful of the sacrifices borne by our ancestors. I thank President Bush for his service to our nation, as well as the generosity and cooperation he has shown throughout this transition.

Forty-four Americans have now taken the presidential oath. The words have been spoken during rising tides of prosperity and the still waters of peace. Yet, every so often the oath is taken amidst gathering clouds and raging storms. At these moments, America has carried on not simply because of the skill or vision of those in high office, but because We the People have remained faithful to the ideals of our forbears, and true to our founding documents.

So it has been. So it must be with this generation of Americans.

That we are in the midst of crisis is now well understood. Our nation is at war against a far-reaching network of violence and hatred. Our economy is badly weakened, a consequence of greed and irresponsibility on the part of some, but also our collective failure to make hard choices and prepare the nation for a new age. Homes have been lost, jobs shed, businesses shuttered. Our health care is too costly, our schools fail too many, and each day brings further evidence that the ways we use energy strengthen our adversaries and threaten our planet.

These are the indicators of crisis, subject to data and statistics. Less measurable but no less profound is a sapping of confidence across our land—a nagging fear that America's decline is inevitable and that the next generation must lower its sights.

Obama needed to help Chief Justice John Roberts when he reversed some words of the oath of office, misplacing the word "faithfully." Obama didn't finish taking the oath until 12:05, five minutes after he actually became president under the Constitution.

Today I say to you that the challenges we face are real. They are serious and they are many.

They will not be met easily or in a short span of time. But know this, America—they will be met. On this day, we gather because we have chosen hope over fear, unity of purpose over conflict and discord.

On this day, we come to proclaim an end to the petty grievances and false promises, the recriminations and worn out dogmas, that for far too long have strangled our politics.

We remain a young nation, but in the words of Scripture, the time has come to set aside childish things. The time has come to reaffirm our enduring spirit; to choose our better history; to carry forward that precious gift, that noble idea, passed on from generation to generation: the God-given promise that all are equal, all are free, and all deserve a chance to pursue their full measure of happiness.

In reaffirming the greatness of our nation, we understand that greatness is never a given. It must be earned. Our journey has never been one of short-cuts or settling for less. It has not been the path for the faint-hearted—for those who prefer leisure over work or seek only the pleasures of riches and fame. Rather, it has been the risk-takers, the doers, the makers of things—some celebrated but more often men and women obscure in their labor—who have carried us up the long, rugged path towards prosperity and freedom.

For us, they packed up their few worldly possessions and traveled across oceans in search of a new life.

For us, they toiled in sweatshops and settled the West, endured the lash of the whip and plowed the hard earth.

For us, they fought and died in places like Concord and Gettysburg, Normandy and Khe Sahn. Time and again these men and women struggled and sacrificed and worked till their hands were raw so that we might live a better life. They saw America as bigger than the sum of our individual ambitions, greater than all the differences of birth or wealth or faction.

This is the journey we continue today. We remain the most prosperous, powerful nation on Earth. Our workers are no less productive than when this crisis began. Our minds are no less inventive, our goods and services no less needed than they were last week or last month or last year. Our capacity remains undiminished. But our time of standing pat, of protecting narrow interests and putting off unpleasant decisions—that time has surely passed. Starting today, we must pick ourselves up, dust ourselves off, and begin again the work of remaking America.

For everywhere we look, there is work to be done. The state of our economy calls for action, bold and swift, and we will act—not only to create new jobs, but to lay a new foundation for growth. We will build the roads and bridges, the electric grids and digital lines that feed our commerce and bind us together. We will restore science to its rightful place and wield technology's wonders to raise health care's quality and lower its cost. We will harness the sun and the winds and the soil to fuel our cars and run our factories. And we will transform our schools and colleges and universities to meet the demands of a new age. All this we can do. And all this we will do.

Now, there are some who question the scale of our ambitions—who suggest that our system cannot tolerate too many big plans. Their memories are short. For they have forgotten what this country has already done—what free men and women can achieve when imagination is joined to common purpose and necessity to courage.

What the cynics fail to understand is that the ground has shifted beneath them—that the stale political arguments that have consumed us for so long no longer apply. The question we ask today is not whether our government is too big or too small, but whether it works—whether it helps families find jobs at a decent wage, care they can afford, a retirement that is dignified. Where the answer is yes, we intend to move forward. Where the answer is no, programs will end. And those of us who manage the public's dollars will be held to account—to spend wisely, reform bad habits, and do our business in the light of day—because only then can we restore the vital trust between a people and their government.

Nor is the question before us whether the market is a force for good or ill. Its power to generate wealth and expand freedom is unmatched, but this crisis has reminded us that without a watchful eye, the market can spin out of control—and that a nation cannot prosper long when it favors only the prosperous. The success of our economy has always depended not just on the size of our Gross Domestic Product, but on the reach of our prosperity, on our ability to extend opportunity to every willing heart—not out of charity, but because it is the surest route to our common good.

As for our common defense, we reject as false the choice between our safety and our ideals. Our Founding Fathers, faced with perils we can scarcely imagine, drafted a charter to assure the rule of law and the rights of man, a charter expanded by the blood of generations. Those ideals still light the world, and we will not give them up for expedience's sake. And so to all other peoples and governments who are watching today, from the grandest capitals to the small village where my father was born: know that America is a friend of each nation and every man, woman, and child who seeks a future of peace and dignity, and we are ready to lead once more.

Recall that earlier generations faced down fascism and communism not just with missiles and tanks, but with sturdy alliances and enduring convictions. They understood that our power alone cannot protect us, nor does it entitle us to do as we please. Instead, they knew that our power grows through its prudent use; our security emanates from the justness of our cause, the force of our example, the tempering qualities of humility and restraint.

We are the keepers of this legacy. Guided by these principles once more, we can meet those new threats that demand even greater effort—even greater cooperation and understanding between nations. We will begin to responsibly leave Iraq to its people, and forge a hard-earned peace in Afghanistan. With old friends and former foes, we will work tirelessly to lessen the nuclear threat, and roll back the specter of a warming planet. We will not apologize for our way of life, nor will we waver in its defense, and for those who seek to advance their aims by inducing terror and slaughtering innocents, we say to you now that our spirit is stronger and cannot be broken; you cannot outlast us, and we will defeat you.

For we know that our patchwork heritage is a strength, not a weakness. We are a nation of Christians and Muslims, Jews and Hindus—and non-believers. We are shaped by every language and culture, drawn from every end of this Earth, and because we have tasted the bitter swill of civil war and segregation and emerged from that dark chapter stronger and more united, we cannot help but believe that the old hatreds shall someday pass; that the lines of tribe shall soon dissolve; that as the world grows smaller, our common humanity shall reveal itself; and that America must play its role in ushering in a new era of peace.

To the Muslim world, we seek a new way forward, based on mutual interest and mutual respect.

To those leaders around the globe who seek to sow conflict or blame their society's ills on the West—know that your people will judge you on what you can build, not what you destroy. To those who cling to power through corruption and deceit and the silencing of dissent, know that you are on the wrong side of history, but that we will extend a hand if you are willing to unclench your fist.

To the people of poor nations, we pledge to work alongside you to make your farms flourish and let clean waters flow, to nourish starved bodies and feed hungry minds. And to those nations like ours that enjoy relative plenty, we say we can no longer afford indifference to suffering outside our borders, nor can we consume the world's resources without regard to effect. For the world has changed, and we must change with it.

As we consider the road that unfolds before us, we remember with humble gratitude those brave Americans who, at this very hour, patrol far-off deserts and distant mountains. They have something to tell us, just as the fallen heroes who lie in Arlington whisper through the ages.

We honor them not only because they are guardians of our liberty, but because they embody the spirit of service, a willingness to find meaning in something greater than themselves. And yet, at this moment—a moment that will define a generation—it is precisely this spirit that must inhabit us all.

For as much as government can do and must do, it is ultimately the faith and determination of the American people upon which this nation relies. It is the kindness to take in a stranger when the levees break, the selflessness of workers who would rather cut their hours than see a friend lose their job which sees us through our darkest hours. It is the firefighter's courage to storm a stairway filled with smoke, but also a parent's willingness to nurture a child, that finally decides our fate.

Our challenges may be new. The instruments with which we meet them may be new. But those values upon which our success depends—honesty and hard work, courage and fair play, tolerance and curiosity, loyalty and patriotism—these things are old. These things are true. They have been the quiet force of progress throughout our history. What is demanded then is a return to these truths. What is required of us now is a new era of responsibility—a recognition, on the part of every American, that we have duties to ourselves, our nation, and the world, duties that we do not grudgingly accept but rather seize gladly, firm in the knowledge that there is nothing so satisfying to the spirit, so defining of our character, than giving our all to a difficult task.

This is the price and the promise of citizenship.

This is the source of our confidence—the knowledge that God calls on us to shape an uncertain destiny.

This is the meaning of our liberty and our creed—why men and women and children of every race and every faith can join in celebration across this magnificent mall, and why a man whose father less than sixty years ago might not have been served at a local restaurant can now stand before you to take a most sacred oath.

So let us mark this day with remembrance, of who we are and how far we have traveled. In the year of America's birth, in the coldest of months, a small band of patriots huddled by dying campfires on the shores of an icy river. The capital was abandoned. The enemy was advancing. The snow was stained with blood. At a moment when the outcome of our revolution was most in doubt, the father of our nation ordered these words be read to the people:

"Let it be told to the future world... that in the depth of winter, when nothing but hope and virtue could survive... that the city and the country, alarmed at one common danger, came forth to meet [it]."

America, in the face of our common dangers, in this winter of our hardship, let us remember these timeless words. With hope and virtue, let us brave once more the icy currents and endure what storms may come. Let it be said by our children's children that when we were tested we refused to let this journey end, that we did not turn back nor did we falter; and with eyes fixed on the horizon and God's grace upon us, we carried forth that great gift of freedom and delivered it safely to future generations.

"On this day," Obama said in a forceful passage of his address that seemed aimed at the outgoing President Bush, "we gather because we have chosen hope over fear, unity of purpose over conflict and discord. On this day, we come to proclaim an end to the petty grievances and false promises, the recriminations and worn-out dogmas that for far too long have strangled our politics."

Page 6: Reuters/Kevin Lamarque/Landov
Pages 8-9: AP/M. Spencer Green (left); Aurora Photos/Samantha Appleton (center); AP/M. Spencer Green (top right)
Pages 10-11: Reuters/Mike Segar/Landov (left); AP/Charlie Neibergall (center); AP/Ron Edmonds (right)
Pages 12-13: AP/Chicago Tribune/Nancy Stone (top left); Reuters/John Gress/Landov (bottom left); AP/Susan Walsh (center)
Pages 14-15: AP/J. Scott Applewhite (left inset); Reuters/John Gress/Landov
Pages 16-17: AP/Jeff Roberson
Pages 18-19: AP/Kiichiro Sato (left); AP/Rob Carr (right)
Pages 20-21: AP/Evan Vucci
Page 22: UPI/Roger L. Wollenberg/Landov
Pages 24-25: AP/Michael A. Mariant (bottom left); AP/Mannie Garcia (center); Reuters/Fred Prouser/Landov (upper right); UPI/Dennis Brack/Landov (bottom right)
Page 26: AP/M. Spencer Green
Page 29: AP/Nam Y. Huh
Pages 30-31: AP/Manuel Balce Ceneta (bottom left); Aurora Photos/Callie Shell (top left); AP/Pablo Martinez Monsivais (bottom right)
Page 33: AP/Manuel Balce Ceneta (top); Aurora Photos/Callie Shell (bottom right)
Page 35: UPI/Brendan Smialowski/Landov
Pages 36-37: AP/Sayyid Azim (left); Reuters/Radu Sigheti/Landov (center); AP/Sayyid Azim (top right)
Page 38: Reuters/Radu Sigheti/Landov (bottom left); AP/Sayyid Azim
Pages 40-41: Jeff Widener
Page 42: Polaris
Pages 44-45: Associated Press (left); Polaris (right)
Pages 46-50: Jeff Widener
Page 52: Associated Press
Pages 54-59: Jeff Widener
Pages 60-61: Joseph White (left); AP/Tina Fineberg (top left); Bloomberg News/Jennifer S. Altman/Landov (center)
Pages 64-65: AP/M. Spencer Green
Page 67: AP/Nam Y. Huh
Pages 68-69: Polaris (left); AP/Sayyid Azim (center); AP/Karel Prinsloo (bottom right)
Pages 72-73: AP/Chitose Suzuki (top left); Polaris (center and right)
Pages 74-75: AP/Ron Edmonds (left); Newhouse News Service/Landov (top right); AP/Steve Matteo (right)
Page 76: AP/Charlie Neibergall (top); AP/Ed Reinke (bottom)
Pages 78-79: AP/M. Spencer Green
Page 80: AP/M. Spencer Green (top left); AP/State Journal Register/Kevin German (bottom right)
Pages 82-83: AP/Jeff Roberson (left inset); Aurora Photos/Samantha Appleton (center and bottom right)
Page 84: AP/M. Spencer Green
Pages 86-87: Aurora Photos/Callie Shell
Page 88: UPI/Michael Kleinfeld/Landov
Page 90: Aurora Photos/Callie Shell
Pages 92-93: Clockwise from top center: AP/Charlie Riedel; AP/Charlie Neibergall; AP/Kiichiro Sato; Reuters/Lucy Nicholson/Landov; AP/Elaine Thompson
Pages 94-95: Clockwise from top center: AP/Tom Mihalek; AP/Alan Diaz; AP/Mike Derer; AP/Paul Connors; AP/Ron Ira Steele; AP/Alex Brandon
Pages 96-97: Aurora Photos/Callie Shell (left inset and center); AP/Gerald Herbert (right inset)
Pages 98-99: Aurora Photos/Callie Shell
Page 101: AP/Ann Heisenfelt (top left); UPI/Roger L. Wollenberg/Landov (top right); AP/Manuel Balce Ceneta (bottom right)
Pages 102-103: AP/Manuel Balce Ceneta
Page 104: AP/Richard Carson
Pages 106-107: AP/Pablo Martinez Monsivais
Page 109: AP/Obed Zilwa
Page 111: AP/Sayyid Azim (top right); Reuters/Daud Yussuf/Landov
Page 112: AP/Pablo Martinez Monsivais
Pages 114-115: Aurora Photos/Callie Shell (top); AP/Jim Cole (bottom)
Pages 116-117: AP/Evan Vucci (left); AP/M. Spencer Green (right)
Pages 118-119: AP/M. Spencer Green (bottom left); Reuters/Howard Burditt/Landov (top right)
Pages 120-121: AP/Steven Senne (top left); AP/Brian Kersey (bottom)
Pages 122-123: Clockwise from left: UPI/Roger L. Wollenberg/Landov; AP/Jeff Roberson; AP/Jim Cole; Aurora Photos/Callie Shell
Pages 124-125: Polaris (left inset); Fame Pictures (center, top right, bottom right)
Pages 126-127: AP/Jim Cole (top left); Reuters/Brian Snyder/Landov (bottom left); AP/Seth Wenig (right)
Page 128: AP Photo/Charles Rex Arbogas
Page 129: AP Photo/Charles Rex Arbogast (top); Library of Congress
Page 131: AP Photo/Charles Rex Arbogast
Page 132: AP Photo/M. Spencer Green
Page 133: AP Photo/M. Spencer Green
Page 134: AP Photo/M. Spencer Green
Page 136: AP Photo/Matt Rourke
Page 138: AP Photo/Charles Krupa
Page 140: AP Photo/J. Scott Applewhite
Page 142: AP Photo/Brett Flashnick
Page 144: AP Photo/M. Spencer Green
Page 145: Sipa via AP Images
Page 146: Reuters/Mike Segar/Landov
Page 147: Paul Morse/Bloomberg News/Landov
Page 148: AP Photo/Charles Rex Arbogast
Page 149: UPI Photo/Jim Ruymen/Landov
Page 151: AP Photo/Alex Brandon
Page 152: AP Photo/Trinity United Church of Christ
Page 154: AP Photo/Matt Rourke
Page 156: Daniel Barry/Bloomberg News/Landov (top); AP Photo/Carolyn Kaster (bottom)
Page 157: AP Photo/Rick Bowmer
Page 158: AP Photo/Chuck Burton
Page 160: AP Photo/Alex Brandon
Page 161: AP Photo/John Raoux (top); AP Photo/Alex Brandon (bottom)
Page 162: AP Photo/Chris Carlson
Page 165: AP Photo/Ssg. Lorie Jewell HO
Page . 167: AP Photo
Page 168: AP Photo/Ted S. Warren
Page 169: AP Photo/Ron Edmonds (top); AP Photo/ Ron Edmonds (bottom)
Page 171: AP Photo/Gary Hershorn, Pool
Page 172: AP Photo/Jane C. Hong (top); AP Photo/Charles Knoblock (bottom)
Page 174: AP Photo/Alex Brandon (left); AP Photo/Morry Gash (top right); AP Photo/Stephan Savoia (bottom right)
Page 175: AP Photo/Morry Gash
Page 176: AP Photo/The White House, Eric Draper
Page 177: AP Photo/Gerald Herbert (top); AP Photo/J. Scott Applewhite (bottom)
Page 178: AP Photo/Gerald Herbert (top); AP Photo/Gerald Herbert (bottom)
Page 181: AP Photo/Jae C. Hong (top); AP Photo/Gerald Herbert (bottom)
182: AP Photo/Obama Transition Office, Callie Shell
183: AP Photo/Richard Drew
184: AP Photo/Susan Walsh
185: AP Photo/Alex Brandon
187: AP Photo/Susan Walsh (top); AP Photo/Saul Loeb, Pool (right); AP Photo/Alex Brandon (bottom right); AP Photo/Charles Dharapak (bottom)
188: AP Photo/Jae C. Hong
191: AP Photo/Jae C. Hong